Cont

Cuba: A Tourist's Paradise

So, you've decided to visit Cuba...Hola! In our opinion, you have made a great choice.

In many ways, Cuba is a perfect destination for a wide range of tourists. Despite the warped perception of Cuba that is formed by what many people have heard about Cuba's historic tensions with the United States, which has created a lot of confusion and skepticism regarding the beautiful island nation as an option for tourists, Cuba will surely please you. Rest assured, you will not be disappointed with the time you spend in this fabulous country, and you will almost certainly be surprised by the fruits of the land, literally and figuratively.

Cuba is a spectacular destination, full of all of the beautiful splendors that are associated with tropical Caribbean island life, as well as a wealth of unique quirks that add a welcome splash of colour to the visitor experience.

Due to an interesting mixture of the nation's storied past, current and persisting reformed po-litical identity, and geographical location, Cuba has become an incredibly unique country: a Spanish-influenced tropical paradise that exists as a socialist republic, free from the direct influence of many Western powers. The journey has not been easy for Cuba, but this small nation with a huge passion for liberty has managed to succeed beyond what many would have projected.

Cuba is a spectacular destination, full of all of the beautiful splendors

Today, the country is renowned for its vivid, strong, and diverse culture. This can be seen in many facets of Cuban life. The wild nightlife in the major city of Havana is world famous; the infectious Afro-Cuban rumba music bursts out of vibrant bars and music halls, the tropical rum flows freely and affordably, and the busy streets run rampant with retro-American

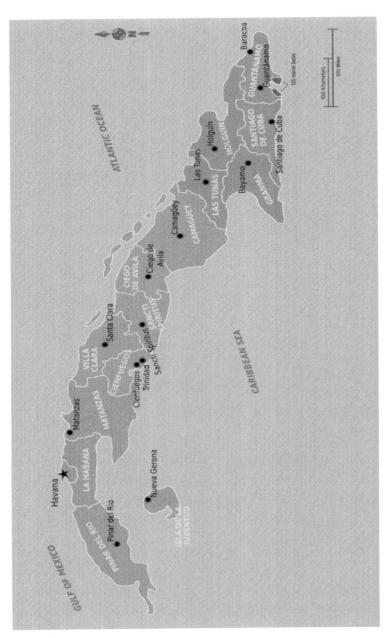

4

Chrysler, Buick, and Ford classic cars that are typically from the 1950s. In the experience of many seasoned travelers, another place that carries the same distinct charms as Cuba has certainly not yet been experienced. And yet, many areas of Cuba contrast this greatly; quaint villages tucked away in the mountainous green, and quiet seaside beach-towns in which the only sounds are the songs of birds and the ocean's gentle breeze.

Despite the wonderful and wild energy of Havana, and the bright vitality of the hidden beauty scattered around the rest of the country, a trip to this island is not necessarily one without a few complications. Luckily, the most severe obstacles are faced by visitors from one nation only: yes, any difficulties are especially enhanced for American citizens, who have a notoriously difficult time vacationing in Cuba due to the strict visa rules and regulations placed by their own government. This regulation stems from the infamous tension that has existed between the two countries for what has become more than one-

half of a century, dating back to issues that relate to the Cold War. Generally, no animosity is held by Cuban citizens towards American visitors, but the governments of these two countries have been at odds with each other for over 50 years, and the hoops that an American citizen must jump through to make their way to Cuba certainly strip some simplicity from the process.

In this guide, we will take a look at what makes Cuba what it is today-- examining the island nation from several different perspectives. First and foremost, this guide aims to communicate one basic message: if you are interested in going to Cuba, quit with the hesitation! Buy a ticket and take the ride! And for the others, who are seemingly not interested in visiting this unique island nation... why not!? You should be! There is nothing not to love!

Cuba is a vastly underrated tourist destination that features many of the best and most beloved attributes from the world's most popular locations and hotspots-- however, it does not always get the justified credit that it deserves for being a premier location, seemingly for a variety of strange reasons. In many ways this is not necessarily a bad thing, as it keeps the tourism industry at a healthy level that does not jeopardize Cuba's true culture; from another perspective, it is about time that Cuba starts getting more respect. That is what we aim to do with this guide: shed light upon the beauty of Cuba and spread the word of its merit.

As we move through this guide together, we will delve deeper into the following topics: Cuba's history, culture, appeal for tourists, wide range of activities and entertainment, and more.

History of Cuba

Although it would be easy to quantify the tourist experience in dreamy Cuba with nothing more than local rum, classic Chrysler cars, iconic images of Che Guevara, exotic live music, and general sun soaking-- this surface level interpretation would only begin to tell the island nation's compelling story. Yes, these are popular elements of the culture, and surely contribute to Cuba's beloved identity. However, there are some elements of the history of this odd outlier of a socialist paradise that can enlighten your perspective and enrich the time you spend in the country.

In the late 15th century, Christopher Columbus made his way to what is now known as Cuba and gave the island the title of "Juana." The name comes from the title of Prince Don Juan, and was a direct tribute to the famous son of Queen Isabella of Castile. What we now know as Cuba was possessed and "owned" by several different colonial empires; power shifted in fluctuation as the Spanish, English, and American imperialists were continually struggling over ownership of the land. Three-and-a-half years after the Spanish-American war, which culminated with Cuba being possessed by the American military, Cuba finally became its

" "

Cuba was possessed and "owned" by several different colonial empires

own Republic in 1902.

In the 1950's, Fidel and Raul Castro staged a famous revolution with the help of Che Guevara and the support of legions of Cubans. They overthrew the Batista government with their communist party and began governing the island nation as a

"

The "embargo" was put in place to intensely restrict commercial and financial transactions

socialist state. The nation continues to function in this way to this day, despite over half of a century's worth of serious resistance from the United States of America.

Relations with the USA

In 2017, the story between Cuba and the USA continues to be one that is full of twists, turns, and turbulence. In 2014, former President Barack Obama began to deconstruct the trade and travel embargo that had existed between the nations since the 1950's, perhaps at its most intense during the Cold War in 1961. American federal resistance to Cuba was rejuvenated by President Donald J Trump and the Republican Party of America in 2017.

It should be noted that the people of Cuba are quite hospitable towards Americans who visit their country, as this struggle is mostly to do with federal politics-- not individual citizens. America's political resentment toward Cuba stems directly from the Cuban revolution of 1959, in which the Castro brothers overthrew the Batista regime, which had deep allegiances to the United States. The "embargo" was put in place to intensely restrict commercial and financial transactions, such as trade, between the United States and Cuba. After over 50 years of stagnation and resentment, Barack Obama initiated "the Cuban thaw" which began to ease the restrictions placed on Cuba by the United States. This agreement saw initiatives meant to revamp travel and tourism between the countries. It would allow citizens of the two countries to visit with far less work and bureaucratic effort, as well as renegotiating remittances, beginning to re-open trade, and generally creating a healthier relationship between the nations and their populations. However, opposition to Cuban diplomacy is still powerful within certain segments of American society, as witnessed by Donald Trump's "canceling" of Obama's agreements with Cuba.

Progress in this matter is slow and steady. Travel to Cuba is still an option though, and by all accounts-- it is a great one. For Americans, more work is certainly required, though the common opinion is a simple one: it's worth the effort!

Current Conditions for American Tourists

Cuba may not be as easy to access for some travelers as other locations. But it's still a possibility.

As of President Donald Trump's decree in June of 2017, travel restrictions to Cuba are once again intensified and progress toward civility between these nations has been halted and reversed. The impacts of this proclamation will act as an obstacle, but not a "wall" in terms of preventing Americans from entering the country as a tourist. Technically, the "ban" to allow American tourists into Cuba was never lifted, but certain accommodations were made to create access options for curious Americans.

The new rules say quite

simply that: "(the) traveler's schedule of activities must not include free time or recreation in excess." Obama created 12 legal ways of travelling to Cuba. The important distinction to make in this regard is the separation of "travel" and "tourism". The biggest change that Trump's administration has made is creating a "ban" on people entering Cuba on educational or cultural excursions that have been planned privately.

It is quite possible that the easiest and best way for Americans to access Cuba will be as a member of a tour group. These tour groups are organized by tour operators with specific licenses... Also, the following channels of travel are still considered to be valid:

-Family travel (the allowance for Americans to visit their families in Cuba)
    -professional research and meetings
    -religious activities
    -humanitarian projects
    -public performances
(for artists, athletes, and performers)

If you feel as though your trip can qualify as suitable by fitting into one of these categories: perfect. If not, there is no reason to be afraid. There are travel agencies that specialize in finding ways to facilitate a Cuban experience for Americans who will know precisely what is best for you.

It is unfortunate that these restrictions currently they exist, but they are not blocks on the road as much as they are bumps.

Cuba facts

Cuba has a 99.8% literacy rate, which is one of the highest in the world

10 Reasons For A Tourist To Visit Cuba

Cuba is more than just "an island in the Caribbean", it stands distinctly apart from many other tropical vacation options. Sure, it is true: Cuba may not be as easy to access for some travelers as other locations. Still, even for those travelers: we would suggest that it is worth jumping through a few extra hoops to get a taste of what Cuba has to offer.

You may be "on the fence" about visiting Cuba. This is understandable; the world is full of amazing places that have all sorts of wonderful elements that make them special.

15

However, this does not mean Cuba should not be overlooked. In fact, Cuba stands out as unique from every other country that is even remotely similar.

Visiting Cuba is a life changing decision that creates memories that simply can't be replicated anywhere else in the world!

So, what makes Cuba so special?

Here are 10 things that make choosing Cuba worthwhile!

10. The Weather

Cuba is nestled within the Caribbean Tropic of Cancer. This creates a joyously tropical climate that creates a high warmth that is hardly ever im-

pacted by cool winds and rains. November to April generally features less rain than May to October, but there is some fluidity within this. The weather is not unbearably hot and we can say with certainty that it never-- and we mean NEVER-- gets cold. The result of this is a pleasant stability that has less variance than many other countries. In the midst of the winter, the average temperature is 21 °C (69.8 °F), while the general summer temperature is roughly 27 °C (80.6 °F). Consider the most popular, beloved temperature for humans is generally considered to be roughly 23 °C (73.4 °F), Cuba presents a compelling argument for being one of the most ideal locations and climate zones to vacation within on the planet.

Cuba is extremely humid, which can intensify the way that these temperatures feel, but it is absolutely within reason. The oceans around the country represent great swimming opportunities on beautiful beaches and air-conditioning is ever-present, so the country is well-equipped for soothing any extremes in heat that the tourist may feel.

Cuba is ideal for those who like their weather "hot" but not "too hot."

9. A Unique Exposure to Socialist Society

Despite intense pressure from external forces, Cuba continues to thrive as a socialist nation. Citizens of Cuba take great pride in their country's identity, and the differences between socialist society and capitalist society are everywhere! There are tributes to historical figures such as Marx and Lenin everywhere, for example. You will also notice that the "billboards" in Cuba generally feature positive, progressive political messages rather than product

advertisements. Cuba is a living list of the pros and cons of living within communism and socialism rather than capitalism, and the differences are stark! Cuba ranks very highly in world rankings for health care, education, and sustainable development in compliance with nature. They even offer their medical school post-secondary programs for free to keep their top notch healthcare running like a well-oiled machine! However, there are downsides, and Cuba's lack of access to an abundance of food supplies creates a situation where anybody who helps you will almost always prefer you to buy them a nutritious snack rather than give them a dollar.

Even if you are not a fan of socialist systems, exposing yourself to such a unique culture is still very interesting and certainly

provides some food for thought!

The system itself is not necessarily a reason to visit, but the effects that socialism has on a country are quite pronounced and should be experienced first-hand. Whatever your opinion is, and no matter how strong it is, there is nothing like an immersive experience to add depth to your philosophy on any matter.

8. Affordability and Availability Of The "Finer Things" (Alcohol)

Many travel locations are deceptively expensive because of the ingredients that are often utilized to have a good, fun, and loose time in the evening (also known as partying). Cuba is not one of these places and does not suffer from this problem. Rather the opposite, actually. For

19

your average adult traveler, the low price on popular treats such as alcohol will surely be appreciated. In Cuba, it is possible to purchase a decent beer for 1 or 2 dollars! More than this, public drinking is totally legal in Cuba, and you are more than welcome to wander the streets with a beer in hand, as long as you are doing so in a respectful manner. These beers can be purchased at the frequently encountered state-run stores and it is very common to see travelers and tourists wandering the streets or sitting in the park while enjoying a cool beer.

But what is a trip to Cuba without a few "samples" of their famous rum? Fortunately, rum-based cocktails are also extremely affordable in Cuba! There are all sorts of classic Cuban cocktails to be sampled, many of which are mixed with Havana Club: Cuba's pride and joy of a flagship rum. When in Cuba, drink as the Cubans drink!

Cubans are proud of their rum-culture; it is definitely something to dip into while you engage with Cuba's cultural offerings. Don't miss the opportunity to enjoy a Mojito or a "Cuba Libre" (rum and coke) in the home from which these iconic mixes were born.

7. An Unspoiled Beauty

Yes, if there is one massive benefit to the lack of American presence in Cuba, it would be that Cuba is one of the only countries in the world that is largely free from the presence of American corporations. Unlike so much of the planet, you can stroll through entire cities in Cuba and not find a single McDonalds, KFC, or Starbucks. In their place? Local eateries serving a variety of cuisine, undeterred by the competition of multi-national conglom-

21

erates. Not only does this socialist approach have an impact on the cities and businesses of the country, but on the nature and landscapes of Cuba itself. Less foreign investment means that the tourism industry has not had as significant of an impact on the nation's wondrous natural environments. Cuba is beginning to change, as hotels and other such tourism infrastructure have been seeing a boost in production, specifically after travel restrictions for Americans began the "thawing" process in 2015 and 2016. For anybody who has travelled the world before, the appeal of an authentic cultural setting that can be traversed without seeing the smiling face of Colonel Sanders or the "golden arches" of McDonalds is surely a refreshing thought!

It would be wise to get to Cuba before more trade deals are negotiated and

these extremely popular American companies begin showing their faces.

6. The Nature

It would be unjust to speak of Cuba without mentioning the natural beauty that serves as the foundation for the nation. Whether you are a hiker, a biker, a camper, a lover of water sports, or just someone who enjoys resting in a hammock on the beach, Cuba offers something for you! There is a broad range of landscapes and natural environments to encounter, explore, and dwell within. Cuba's mountains are some of the most underrated and beautiful in the world, emerging triumphantly from tropical forests, full of lush life. Caves and rock formations give clues to the way the local indigenous once lived.

Cuba's beaches are world famous for their majestic Caribbean presence. These beaches sport fine

white-blonde sand that meets up with clean, crystal blue and turquoise Atlantic waters. There are no beaches in the world that quite compare with these fine Caribbean sands; the beaches of Cuba are among the planet's best, combining their perfect physical beauty with idyllic temperatures of the air and water. Get ready to dive in and explore the natural perfection offered up by this island gem.

5. The Cigars

Cuban cigars have quite a solid reputation. When you ask the professionals, there is a pretty clear consensus: they have absolutely earned their sterling reputation. In Cuba, you can buy some of the best cigars in the world directly

from the famous factories that are responsible for creating the products that have gained such international acclaim. In many Cuban stores and factories, you can buy these incredibly hand-rolled products in mass quantities. They are great for adding luxury, leisure, and cultural immersion to your visit to Cuba, but they are also great souvenirs to bring home; Cuban cigars can work great as gifts for all sorts of people in your life!

The best thing about buying Cuban cigars from the source is that they are affordable and you know they will be good quality. A tour or a trip to a major factory in Havana is likely the most efficient and effective way of buying a solid quantity of high-quality smokables.

4. The Cars

For anybody who is a car buff, or who is vaguely interested in "vintage vehicle" culture, Cuba offers a very interesting perk. After the international trade freeze, Cuba simply stopped importing American vehicles. The consequence of this action has been interesting and aesthetically stunning. In Cuba, almost every vehicle you see is a 1950's American make and model, which is generally considered to be the "golden age" of automobile production in the country.

The cars have such a distinct flare that the streets of the cities begin to look like a blast from the past; the traveler begins to feel as if they have gone back to a simpler time. This dreamy sensation is unparalleled in terms of a tourist's experience.

If you wonder how the cars keep running, that is a good question! Mechanics in Cuba have found all sorts of creative ways to repair and refurbish these classic automobiles, even though they have not had access to many of the replacement parts that would generally be used by the American manufacturers. This level of ingenuity is impressive in itself, and the results are absolutely splendid!

3. Vintage Culture

Beyond the vehicles, Cuba also lacks many of the first world amenities and fashionable products that people all over the planet have grown accustomed to, which creates an interesting range of relics in the form of goods and features all over the country. Some continue to criticize the lack of modernity within the economy, while many praise the country for remaining loyal to what works for them.

The presence of many modern technologies that we have become accustomed to is severely limited and sparse in Cuba. There are not many iPhones, laptops, or other ultra-modern devices. Although some see this as a disadvantage, the lack of commonplace technology in day-to-day life has some very interesting impacts on Cuban society. The presence of older, antiquated technologies furthers the old-school charm that is felt in so many ways in the cities, towns, and villages.

This unique, functional approach truly abides by the "if it is not broke, don't fix it" philosophy, and this impacts the Cuban culture in many different ways! One walk through almost any town, city, or village and you will surely notice some oddities and eccentricities which

2. Song & Dance

Havana has a specific reputation for boisterous, booming Afro-Cuban music burning up the lounges, bars, and halls of the city. Amazing music

is present all over Cuba, however, and there is no way that you will be able to keep yourself from moving with the strong, powerful rhythms that define the nation's musical taste. Many people are sur-prised, however, that the music in Cuba is incredibly diverse, and runs beyond the typical rumba music that we typically associ-ate with the country. The streets are filled with the energy of performers, as

27

are the bars and clubs, with everything from jazz to hip-hop and rap, and the sounds of everywhere between South America, Africa, and Spain finding creative ways to be represented. It is not hard to find pure representations of all of these styles, as well as all sorts of unique combinations.

Cuba is a country filled with vibrant music and an urge to follow the beat with an equally exciting diversity of styles of dance. Although there are many different types of dancing that commonly occur in Cuba, there are certainly some similarities-- for example, the dance forms are filled with one minimum requirement: passion! Beyond this, you will also notice that many of the dances are quite complicated and intricate, and many Cubans have the ability to perform these steps at an impressive level. The traditional group dances of Cuba are wide-

ly taught and beloved by Cuba's citizens; the results are fantastic. Big groups can seemingly perform these distinctly choreographed dances with utter expertise! The rumba, guaguanco, congas, salsa, mambo, and cha cha cha dances of Cuba are quite a sight to behold when performed by the exciting locals-- whether they are professional or not!

1. The People

The people of Cuba have earned a reputation for being some of the friendliest and kindest people in the world. They are extremely warm and generous with time, resources, and hospitality in general. Cubans are known for being very open to conversation and forming positive relationships with tourists. They are also, generally, very social. The cities and towns of Cuba are filled with people enjoying life; playing sports, conversing with each other, and

enjoying the fresh air while walking or riding bicycles. The social scene is alive and well, and it certainly serves as a stark contrast to many societies where travelers come from, in which people are competitive and cut off from each other. In Cuban culture, nothing is more important than maintaining healthy relations with friends and family; Cubans are incredibly supportive and loving people. Many travelers speak of the unparalleled friendliness, warmth, generosity, and lively humor that so many Cu-

bans seem to effortlessly possess.

Socializing, in general, plays a bigger part in day to day life in the active Cuban citizen. It is a beautiful thing to witness, and Cubans are not stingy about who they offer their energy to; the relationship between locals and tourists is among the most special on the planet. The lack of an excess of technology is one reason that this is the case, as people do not depend on their phones, devices, and products to fill their social requirements, they depend on each other.

Finally, Cubans are some of the most honest and trustworthy locals in a tourist setting that you can imagine. Very few people are looking to swindle tourists and most people would return your wallet or expensive item you have left behind, maybe asking no more than just a meal purchased in return for the deed, or less. It is very important to Cubans that visitors leave with a positive impression of the country that they are so proud to be from.

Cuban Cuisine

cuisine that defines the national flavor of the country in a way that is not specific to restaurants.

Though there are obviously certain restaurants in specific towns, cities, neighborhoods, and areas, there is some Cuban

Many people come back from Cuba saying that the lack of extremely delicious food is the one thing holding the country back from

becoming a truly top-tier tourist destination.

We disagree with this, however. Cuba does have a more distinct relationship to its food than many of its competitors within the tourism industry, largely because of trade restrictions and self-sufficiency in creating a lot of its own supply of ingredients.

Let's set the record straight here. The food in Cuba is in no way unappealing. It is well-made and it is typically made from entirely organic ingredients. Is the cuisine as refined (and defined) as Italian, Mexican, or any of the Far East countries? Probably not. Does it pale in comparison to other Caribbean nations? Some think so, I don't necessarily. The flavours are not as strong as Jamaican jerk, for example, but the national foods do have an understated deliciousness to them, in our opinion.

Here is what Cuban food is not:

Spicy. For many, this is exciting. For others, it is annoying. This is just the way the cookie crumbles though, is it not? However, this is not just true in the sense of "hot" spicy food-- in Cuba, spices are sparsely used in general. This means that the food is not extremely flavourful. But it is hearty, healthy, and still quite tasty-- and it is almost always well prepared!

Another exciting thing about Cuban cuisine is that there is not an extensive amount of it, so a short trip to Cuba of only a couple of weeks could potentially show you enough about the food to have a very informed perspective.

As the economy begins to modernize and adapt though, as does the culinary palate of the nation, and some interesting developments are beginning to occur; in general, it seems very possible that Cuban food is in a state of reinventing itself. This is exciting.

The US embargo and trade restrictions with Cuba severely limit their range of ingredients in certain seasons or when it comes to some specific ingredients. In the world of importing goods, in today's day and age, the USA is not the most ideal nation to have an adversarial relationship with. The biggest issue, with this in mind, is consistency. Sometimes restaurants just can't supply certain dishes that require certain ingredients, which is not an issue that most other countries face.

Still, Cuba finds a way to cope and adapt, and one of the ways they do this is by working with simple, core dishes that can be prepared with consistency. Many restaurants will go through phases where they are not able to serve everything on their menu, but this is just accepted as a necessary consequence of the current state of affairs in Cuba.

Cuba's lack of capitalism helps in terms of ethical eating, however. For those who care about animal rights, Cuba represents a nice dynamic. The animals are generally not treated with the adverse conditions of factory farming, and the meat and produce both benefit from a lack of artificial additives. In the past, Cuba has worked hard at creating methods that allow them to practice farming in an environmentally responsible and ecologically sound way, which allows them to enhance sustainability as well as enhance the flavour of their foods through the benefit of allowing their food to be natural.

Cuban Cuisine: Eating Out

First thing is first: when eating at one of Cuba's state-run restaurants or cafes, you should expect to have to pay in cash. Generally the food is very affordable and many places do not have the necessary infrastructure to accept cards of any variety... Many more expensive places that cater specifically to tourists will take credit cards, but it is still better to be safe and carry cash. You don't have to worry about being robbed or mugged in Cuba like you do in a lot of other popular tourist destinations. There is no downside to carrying enough cash to afford your daily meals, and it can make things much simpler.

There are a few different types of places to eat in most Cuban cities and towns. There are convertible-peso and national-peso eateries. They are both run by the state, and they have very different vibes. Generally, the convertible-peso places are catered towards tourists, and the food is of a better quality. That is not necessarily true though. Some places manage to be very inexpensive for locals and also rather delicious.

A lot of the places that are meant for locals though just serve Cuban food prepared very simply. At the same time, a lot of the eateries and restaurants that are aimed towards tourists delve into a Cuban take on international foods; there is Italian food, Chinese food, and

Cuba facts

Cuba is often called El Caiman (Spanish for alligator), which is what the island looks like from an aerial view

more to be found in urban centres such as Havana. Is it great? Some of it is!

It is hard to generalize the food in Cuba because it ranges so greatly-- their food system is unique just like so many of their other systems seem to be.

If you are picky about your food and do not feel like taking risks when you travel, you may want to stick to the restaurants that are actually located within tourism centres and hotels. These places will often serve pizza

and pasta that are tasty but unspectacular. They are likely not as good as the pizza and pasta you love back home, but can ground your culinary experience in something familiar, if you are the type of person who prefers that type of situation.

Like every other aspect of tourist-based relations, you will notice that service is almost overly-polite in the state-run establishments, even in the ones that are remarkably inexpensive… Cuba places a high priority on treating people good, and you may be taken off guard by how pleasant and polite the staff members make an effort to be.

Is it worth checking out the national-peso restaurants?

In our opinion, absolutely!

This is basic Cuban food that is typically consumed by the locals and it is not exactly the most exciting food. Cubans are quite conservative with spice and their relationship with food is much different than that of many Western nations. The experience of eating at one of these state-run places is still an interesting and beneficial one, though.

The prices should be converted to your pesos, and you should be able to eat for the exact same low rate as the locals. If you do go, go early. The best stuff goes quick, so it's best to get there before the rush and try the dish that seems to be flying off the shelf the fastest.

Cuban Cuisine: Paladars

This is a very special element of being a tourist in Cuba. Though private enterprise was very much restricted for a long time, Cuba citizens made their desire to earn money through extra work known, and the government responded. So, for over 20 years, individuals have been allowed to pay locals to eat home-cooked meals that are literally cooked, and served, in the homes of locals. They are like small, independent restaurants that are quite literally Mom & Pop shops. The experience of eating at a Paladar is an unforgettable one and many of these serve food that is unparalleled by the state-run cafeterias that are so commonly found throughout the country. This is a developing industry in Cuba, but it is a freedom that the people have embraced and made great progress within. There are a lot of people who are passionate about cooking food in Cuba who previously had no way of sharing their gifts in a sustainable way; now, that has changed, and the tourism industry is beginning to compensate the Cubans who do this quite handsomely. As more and more restrictions have been lifted, Paladars have grown in a meaningful way, and the quality of this style of food has liberated itself and begun to show itself as some of the best food in the country in many settings.

There are a lot of people who are passionate about cooking food in Cuba

It would not be an over-statement to suggest that this is the best way to sample high-quality Cuban cuisine. Howev-

er, as the Paladar scene grows, it has naturally found ways of offering all sorts of cuisines-- there are now a wide variety of

41

options available around the country. It is not difficult to find many types of ethnic food offered in these homes, often in highly stylized and widely appreciated home-settings that have begun to take on great decor and stimulating themes. To separate their paladars from the rest, many practitioners of this emerging dining experience have started to experiment with a diverse array of themes and styles. This has led to a lot of creative and inventive settings that create distinct environments and lead to simply unforgettable dining experiences that are beautifully personal and intimate. Naturally, the variety in paladars leads to a variety within the range of prices. Typically a meal will not cost the tourist more than $10 CUC but, at the same time, the higher end paladars have started to charge as much as $25 CUC for a meal. This is not an extreme price, especially for Westerners, but in comparison to the typical price of a meal in Cuba this is an enormous amount more.

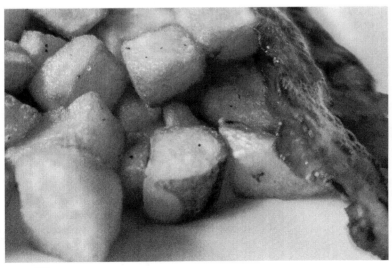

Cuban Cuisine: Genuine, Authentic Local Food

Cuban food has a specific name: comida criolla.
The formula is pretty simple, though it is sometimes
changed. Mostly, comida criolla is based on a few fun-
damental ingredients. Generally, either pork or chicken
is used as a base. The meat will be fried or prepared by
roasting. The classic side for almost every dish served
in Cuba? Rice and beans. In the Cuban diet, rice and

43

beans are the epitome of a staple. They also include "viandas" which may sound exotic and foreign to you, but really this is just what root vegetables are called in Cuba.

There are not that many different local dishes, but some should not be missed if you want to say you've been to Cuba and tasted the food:

Ropa Vieja is a major staple in the Cuban diet, and it has been for a long time-- over 500 years, as a matter of fact. Understanding Ropa Vieja leads to a deeper appreciation for Cuban culture. It has a lot to do with Cuba's present, as well as its past. Originally a Spanish dish, Ropa Vieja translates directly to "old clothes", strangely enough. The mythology behind the food is that a poor man shredded his own clothing as a meal to feed his starving family. He added other common elements from the land and the dish turned into this tasty stew... Is it a real story? Probably not, but who knows. What are the real facts? Less fun, but

still interesting. Ropa Vieja was created on the Iberian peninsula by Sephardic Jews. Typically it consists of beef and stewed vegetables.

Pescado en Escabeche is another Spanish descendent that many different colonies of the country have developed their own take on. Cuba's version is as unique and distinct as the rest of the takes on this dish, if not more. Literally, "Pescado en Escabeche" translates to "pickled fish." In general, Pescado en Escabeche is one of Spain and Latin America's most ancient recipes. It was practical then, in the days before refrigeration, due to the great journeys required to achieve conquest. Now, it is still enjoyed as a staple in many countries, including Cuba. It still does not need to be refrigerated, but it is also simply delicious. Many Cubans will make this dish in large quantities as, when refrigerated, this is a dish that can last for over two weeks. Typically, the ingredients include king-fish steak, onion, paprika, olive oil, peppers, pimento-stuffed olives, and a bay leaf with Spanish sherry vinegar.

Torticas de Moron are deeply beloved Cuban sugar cookies. As far as casual snacks go in Cuba, few sugary sweets are as intimately appreciated as Torticas de Moron. As you may be able to tell, Torticas de Moron come from the central Cuban city of Moron. Who would have thunk? These cookies are really something else, though. They are shortbread cookies that are sprinkled with sugar and carry with them a huge hint of lime and, typically, the inclusion of guava or lemon flavor as well. They pair beautifully with strong coffee, as is typical in Cuba. Other flavours, such as vanilla, rum, or chocolate are sometimes added as well- when this happens, the results can be truly amazing.

Lechon is less likely to stumble upon. In Cuba, Lechon is considered a delicacy. Generally speaking, it is roast pork. But in Cuba it is often done in a very specific way. A popular form of Lechon in Cuba includes marinating the pork in an incredibly delicious sour sauce with strong flavours of garlic and orange.

Fricassee de Pollo; this is another case of a Cuban take on a favourite of many Spanish-influenced nations. Cuba's chicken fricassee is different than many others, such as Mexico's, in one distinct way: can you guess? A lack of spices. The traditional way is this. Peeled chicken with white rice, plantains, and typically served with a freezing malta. Cubano Fricassee de Pollo is a solid, healthy stew that is filled potatoes, olives, and often things like raisins and capers, too.

Cuba Libre is a classic. In most of the world, this is simply called a "rum and coke" but in Cuba, it is so much more than that. In general, it is just a rum and coke-- but, in Cuba, it carries cultural significance. It is a culturally significant caffeinated cocktail that can be made with either light or dark rum and always comes with lime. Don't go to Cuba without ordering a Cuba Libre with some fine Caribbean rum. Yum.

Speaking of cocktails, it would not be a trip to Cuba without an authentic Mojito. The mojito is an internationally famous beverage that was born from Cuba; it consists mostly of lime juice, freshly crushed mint, and (of course) white rum.

Cuban Cuisine: Other Meal Elements

As mentioned, rice and beans are customary in Cuban cuisine. They can come as "congris" which is a mixture of the two, or as "arroz con frijoles." In "arroz con frijoles" the beans and rice are separate from each other. The beans, in this case, are cooked into a stew that has an atypical amount of spice for Cuban food, which is dumped over the rice. It's truly delicious.

> **Try a mamey: a thick, red, fleshy fruit that is often blended into smoothies and shakes**

Fried plantain is a common side in Cuba as well, and is just one way that fruits come into the diet. Fruit also acts as a breakfast staple in Cuba. What fruits are popular in Cuba? Well, whatever is "in season" will be what is for breakfast. Luckily for Cubans, they get some pretty amazing tropical fruits growing down there. Mango, pineapple, oranges, and other tropical fruits become quite commonplace at different times during the year. Try a mamey: a thick, red, fleshy fruit that is often blended into smoothies and shakes. Also, don't miss the opportunity to eat some prickly green soursop if you get the chance-- it is not the most agreeable flavor, but it is totally a thing to do when you are in Cuba-- the taste is both sweet and sour in a wild way that excites the taste buds.

Being an island nation, we would be remiss if we did not mention the availability of fresh seafood. Simply prepared lobster, shrimp, and several varieties of fish make their way onto Cuban dishes in an incredible way. Don't order complicated seafood. Get your fish pan-fried and enjoy the freshness. Trust us, we've been there and done that. When it comes to Cuban seafood: the simpler, the better.

Cuban Cuisine: Food of the Streets

There is serious growth in the Cuban street food scene... Yes, private enterprise has begun to emerge in the form of Street Food in Cuba in a variety of ways. There are food carts and stands on people's property, and storefronts tend to take the shape of anything from a porch to a window to a street trolley.

In our recent experiences in Cuba, there has not been a way of eating that

provides more "bang" for your "buck" -- or more "value" for your "peso". What we mean is that the food is GREAT and very INEXPENSIVE! Such a wonderful combination of things, is it not?

If you are looking for the best option for a type of food that works for a quick snack or an on-the-go lunch-- whether it's because you are on your way somewhere or because you just want to sit in the park and munch on something tasty-- take advantage of the Cuban street food!

As far as lunch and dinner options, there is nothing to scoff at here in this regard, and a lot to sample. All sorts of fried bread and fritters, often paired with freshly concocted scrumptious sauces that can be quite creamy and garlic-based, and one popular street food dish in Cuba is deliciously inexpensive pizza, which is be-

coming increasingly more available from the crafty oft-outdoor vendors.

You must not leave Cuba without trying a local tamale from a street food vendor. The concept is simple: cornmeal, peppers, onions in a wrap made from the leaf of a corn plant. Then? Steam softens the ingredients and gently cooks them together. A spicy red pepper sauce is included to add a burst of flavour if you are the type of person who likes to add a kick to your street food: this is highly recommended in this case.

Cuban Cuisine: Structure of Meals

Dinner is the main meal of the day for the people

49

of Cuba; typically, it will consist of one of the dishes listed above... Some combination of meat, rice, beans, and veggies. For tourists, more options are obviously open with hotel restaurants, paladars, and street food vendors.

Breakfast does not get nearly as much emphasis in Cuba as it does in many western nations. Breakfast is typically a light combination of small portions of bread, eggs, and fruit. Hotel breakfasts will give a few more options, including meat and cereal. We suggest doing your best to adapt to the Cuban style, but if you are stubborn

about meal patterns while traveling, a hearty breakfast option will be provided by most hotels. The main event when it comes to a Cuban breakfast? You guessed it. Coffee. Strong, Cuban coffee with warm milk and sugar.

What's for lunch? For Cubans, lunch is basically just a smaller dose of dinner. The options will be, more or less, the same main course, but will not include any extras.

Sweet Treats

Cuba has always been famous for sugar production and good taste. This seems to have a logical conclusion, does it not? Can you connect the dots here? The sweets, in general, are to die for.

The cakes, cookies, desserts, and ice cream options in Cuba are next-level awesome. The best part? These edible delights are almost always exceptionally affordable-- and they do not rip you off in regards to portion sizes, either. To be honest, the sponge cakes, with generous slabs of meringue, are made of the types of flavours and textures that dreams are made of. I am not exaggerating, Cuban dessert is truly heavenly. These famous meringue-based sponge cakes are so beloved by Cubans that they are gifted to children as birthday gifts by the state. Yes, every child, until the age of 15, gets an amazing birthday gift signed sincerely by the state on an annual basis. No wonder Cubans love their country and their government. Talk about a popularity booster! In all seriousness, this is quite beautiful, as it ensures that children and young people get a nationally-beloved snack on their birthday regardless of their economic standing or familial situation.

Don't miss out on the opportunity to try other treats either: many combinations of shortcake, chocolate, and fruit are waiting to be sampled by the traveler with a sweet tooth, and they are sure to satisfy. Ingredients ranging from coconut to guava, lemon to brown sugar are used, and Cubans are known to combine their sweets with cheese... Have we said "to die for" too much yet? Because when talking about these foods, it is a phrase that wants to come out every second sentence.

Cuban Cuisine: Drink... Alcohol and Beyond

Coffee: Yes. Cuban coffee. If you are a coffee lover,

you have probably been waiting for this. Cuban coffee is quite strong and sweet, and more similar to espresso than your typical American coffee. Cuban coffee is culturally beloved and served almost everywhere. Every restaurant and bar that we could find served this style of coffee, including the most inexpensive national pesos restaurants. Rather than being added after, the addition of sugar occurs while coffee is being made. This gives Cuban coffee its signature appeal, but it also makes it very difficult to buy a coffee that is not sweet-- unless you go to a touristic hotel. By the time you leave, you may not be ready to leave Cuban coffee beans behind, and they make a great souvenir to bring home for others-- and maybe for yourself, too.

There are no hot beverages that even remotely compare to coffee in terms of popularity or cultural significance throughout Cuba. If it were not for tourists, tea would likely not be on the island, and to order tea at a Cuban establishment will likely lead to disappointment for all parties involved. Brewing a pot of tea is not a common strength of any Cuban establishment, as far as we know!

Alcoholic Drinks: Let us begin to discuss the fun stuff (for adults).

Rum. Need I say anything else? Rum is to Cuba what Bourbon is to Tennessee or Vodka is to Russia. Cuban rum has been tried by many, but drinking it in Cuba is a special sensation that all rum enthusiasts, and general alcohol connoisseurs, should be trying. Rum is produced and sold by the state at an incredibly affordable rate: a bottle of rum can be purchased for $3 in many places. A finely crafted cocktail from a hotel, restaurant, or bar will rarely be as expensive as a cool $5. Can you believe it?

We love Havana Club and we are not alone in that. It is a widely beloved national rum. Everybody who loves Cuban rum loves Havana Club-- however, a few competitors are quite popular as well.

Caribbean Club, Siboney, and Santiago de Cuba all have those who are loyal to their brand of rum, too. An inexpensive cocktail will usually be mixed with cheaper white rum, while the finer, darker rums can be enjoyed on their own, or maybe with ice.

Warning: beware of the white street rum. If you hear the words "ron de la calle" you should exercise extreme caution... Only for the reason that those are the last words that many tourists hear before waking up with a hangover for the ages and some blurred memories from the night before. Yes, the street rum is a bit of a right of passage if you are interested in partying, but you will be quite lucky if it is a painless experience. This street rum is distinct. It's viscous and appears to be thicker than your standard rum. Considering a good bottle of rum is about $3, don't let yourself pay that much for the

street stuff. It's cheap, and it deserves to be cheap. This is usually sold on the street, so you should see how inexpensive you can manage to purchase it for, if you are curious regarding this extremely potent beverage.

Sometimes after enough rum (or not enough rum) you feel like enjoying a simple, cold beer. Cristal and Bucanero are beloved Cuban cervezas (beers) that offer their own distinct features. Cristal is light and easy, Bucanero is dark and strong. Beer is sold at state-run corner stores and will usually run less than $3 a drink. You can walk the streets of the cities with a beer in hand if you so choose; there is no legal restriction regarding respectful drinking in public... Just don't get too carried away in public (aka don't be an arse).

Non-Alcoholic Beverages: Not everybody is interested in having an alcohol-infused experience... Yes, apparently some people want to "remember" their vacations. Respectable enough position to take, is it not?

If you fall into this category, or if you are anyone who plans on drinking more than just alcohol, here are some tips that should prove to be quite helpful:

Beer is sold at state-run corner stores and will usually run less than $3 a drink

Tap water should be treated with extreme caution. If you drink water from a tap, make sure it is boiled beforehand. Otherwise, just stick to bottled water if you know what is best for you. Bottled water can be found almost everywhere and it is not particularly expensive.

Do yourself a favor and be responsible for your health by consuming clean water.

Coke and Pepsi are American, familiar brands that have found their way into many state-run shops in Cuba. These 'refrescos' are not expensive and can provide you with the blast of home you may need. However, if you feel adventurous, do not be afraid to sample Cuba's home-grown canned soft drinks, which are quite popular among locals and tourists:

55

-Cachito is a popular canned Cuban lemonade.

-Tropicola is a cola that is not as highly concentrated in regards to the amount of sugar.

-Orangeade is basically what it sounds like but maybe even more intense.

-Malta is a local fizzy drink that is, as the name suggests, quite malty. It takes some getting used to.

-Granizado is a ice-filled, cool, slush-based beverage that you will find being sold from street carts and sold in a paper cone, much like a Sno-Cone.

-Guarapo is a sweet sugar cane based beverage.

-Pru is a bit like ginger beer: fermented in spices and ultra-fresh.

-Lemonade is so readily, affordably available at most establishments that it is hardly even advertised.

Entertainment in Cuba

As touched on previously, entertainment in Cuba often derives from the forms of music and dance which have been developed, born, adopted, or simply experienced unique evolution within the diverse provinces of the island nation. Whether you are being blown away by the vibrant blasts of skilled expression in an exotic Cuban Cabaret (Tropicana) or watching classical guitarists and

instrumentalists improvise in a relaxed park on a Sunday afternoon, the arts and entertainment seem to permeate many different settings and environments all around Cuba.

Still, despite the amount of national pride that infuses many of the forms of expression, each type of Cuban entertainment brings its own set of special parameters. At a Tropicana, you will likely see sultry, adult-driven performances by beautiful dancers and singers, many of whom will be scantily clad and decked out in feathered and ornate costumes. Other forms appear more conservative and traditional, such as the sights that you will see when attending a performance by the Cuban National Ballet. In all truth, neither of these types of aesthetic are 'more' or 'less' Cuban than the other; the spectrum of Cuban arts is simply a broad and diverse one.

Make sure to ask the locals and tourism agencies about seasonal festivals that may be occurring during the time frame of

your visit. There are few ways to get as authentic and enjoyable of a taste of Cuban culture as attending one of their festivals, whether it is old or new. Cuba is a country that is world-famous for the way in which it celebrates, so do your best to attend any festival that you can conceivably find your way to. Whether you are in a small village or a major city, music festivals are worth attending-- in both contemporary and traditional forms.

Latin rhythms and styles manifest in many ways in this country that has arts deriving from African and Spanish, many of which include combinations which have become distinctly Cuban. Visiting Cuba would not be complete without a thorough introduction and immersion into the "arts and culture" section of the country; the emotional understanding that is formed from encountering these forms deepens the intensity and provides more meaning for most of the country's other attractions and offered experiences.

Shopping in Cuba

Shopping is an interesting experience when taking a trip to Cuba. Like most international hot spots, Cuba is equipped with its own souvenirs that simply cannot be replicated by a purchase from anywhere else. Whether you are shopping for yourself,

others, or both, Cuba will certainly have something to offer. Cuba's arts, crafts, and local products have proven to be among the most popular in the entire Caribbean. Major cities sport fashionable shopping centres, and any inhabited area will generally feature specialty shops, artisanal specialists, and outdoor markets. Beyond this, Cuba specializes in a few of the finer things in life, like rum, cigars, and coffee, with such tact and expertise that the nation has emerged as a world leader in these fields.

It is entirely possible that there is no cigar more iconic than a Cuban cigar. All over the country, cigar factories and specialty shops offer amazing discounts on some of the most professionally well-rolled tobacco on the entire planet. Many of the most reputable brands of cigars on the planet still call Cuba their "home" and their plantations, factories, and shops can be visited to this day. You will not find a better deal on Partagas, Montecristo cigars, or Romeo y Julietas in any other country on the planet; seize the day while you are in Cuba and make a purchase on a batch of any of these brands (or others) at an amazing price.

The coffee in Cuba has also earned a special reputation amongst global leaders. The plantations are beautiful to visit, specifically in Pinar del Rio and in the wilderness which surrounds Santiago de Cuba. Treat yourself to a tour of one of the amazing plantations, learn all about harvesting the crop, and do not forget to purchase a bag of beans for yourself either. Don't forget to speak to the locals and drink a lot of coffee as "research" to learn the best way to prepare your cup of coffee when you return home with the beans: Cuban style.

The coffee in Cuba has also earned a special reputation amongst global leaders

We would be remiss if we did not include rum in the category of Cuba's most well-crafted and distinctive products. Cuban rum is beloved all over the

62

world, and Cuba's most widely appreciated cocktails, the Cuba Libre (rum & coke) and the Mojito are among the planet's most consumed alcoholic beverages. Many cities offer tours of their current and historical rum factories, which are very informative if you have any type of interest in the history of alcohol distillation and production, or in Cuba's relationship with its national alcohol.

The Flora and the Fauna

Like everything else we have been associating with Cuba, the flora and fauna of Cuba will display one admirable trait: diversity. Mountains, beaches, coastline, waterfalls, and rivers. Whether you are exploring and adventuring, or just watching out the window as your travel from town to town, Cuba's natural life is truly a treat for the senses. Half of Cuba's 7000 species of plants are endemic and over 75% of the animals are too.

Cuba cares about conservation and this is a gift for locals as well as tourists. Nearly 9000 square kilometres of the land is protected with national conservation, spread around 263 designated areas. There is an impressively low amount of dangerous plants and animals; Cuba's natural wonderland is non-threatening and ready to be engaged with!

Typical Cuban birds include the hummingbird, parakeet, and the flamingo. The reptile life includes crocodiles, boa constrictors, iguanas, and treefrogs. There are lots of bats, too!

There are also over 3000 square kilometres of reef, second only to the Bahamas in the Caribbean.

Havana

Cuban heat brims from this urban centre, which remains culturally cool

The city of Havana is the cultural hub of Cuba; it's the capital city, the largest city, and the centre of arts and commerce. Havana has an otherworldly feel and does not necessarily give off the vibe of being an "urban metropolis" even though over two million people live in the city; this makes Havana the most populated city in the entire Caribbean region. In a Caribbean context, it's 728 square kilometre size (281.18 square miles) is enough to make it the larg-

est sized city in the region as well.

Like a lot of Central and Southern urban areas, there is a predominant Spanish influence on the culture and especially on the architecture of Havana. This Spanish-influenced architecture blends with the vintage American vehicles, the Afro-cuban music, and the unique cultural landscape that emerges from the absence of capitalism in a society makes Havana a true gem of a city.

In terms of an energetic, buzzing city, there is no equivalent to Havana within Cuba; in fact, there are hardly any equivalents within the Caribbean. Not

only is there ample opportunity for shopping and entertainment, but Havana is also the home of almost every major government office, ministry, and business headquarters in all of Cuba.

Even in the face of travel restrictions, tropical Havana is still visited by at least one million travelers on a yearly basis. Havana offers a wide range of features, in our experience, there is something for everybody within this special city.

Havana can be broken down into several neighborhoods, many of which are popular with tourists and travelers, but there are basically three city-sections within Havana. Old Havana is the most popular, Vedado brings its own charms, and then there are outlying suburban districts that are generally newer developments than the older areas of the city.

First, let's take a look at the two city sections that are most appealing to tourists: Old Havana and Vedado.

Old Havana

Old Havana, or "Habana Vieja" as it is called by the locals, is truly the heart of a city that is brimming with life, love, and positive energy. Since 1982, Old Havana has been considered a UNESCO World Heritage Site, which is a major distinction that places an imperative on preserving the architecture and culture of globally unique and significant locations; Old Havana, in our opinion, must have been a "no-brainer" as far as earning this distinction.

Old Havana is the most obvious and blatantly influenced area in terms of the impact of the Spanish colonialism that Cuba was a part of in previous centuries. The appearance of these buildings and how the Spanish layout has evolved, changed, and remained the same is the major contributing factor to United Nations designating this area as a world heritage site.

Not only have buildings been preserved, but there has also been restoration money given by UNESCO with the purpose of maintaining the original beauty of the town. There are other areas that provide a more laid-back and local cultural experience, but for most tourists no area is as popular as Habana Vieja. There is nothing like the wonderful terraces and the booming music that vibrantly fill this part of the city.

Enjoying Old Havana: Plaza Vieja / Catedral

The core of Habana Vieja is generally agreed upon to be the "Plaza Vieja" area, also known as the "Catedral" neighborhood. When the city was fresh and new, the cathedral was absolutely considered

to be the centre of the city, but centuries of expansion have warped that reality ever-so-slightly.

Still, in terms of Havana's pearls and treasures, this area is among the richest. Much like a European city, there are winding cobblestone streets that connect the city's oldest and most significant man-made landmarks; the aforementioned Cathedral, La Fuerza Fortress, El Templete, and the City Museum are the major stops, and between each of them there is typically a wealth of shops and spots to stop. The area is typically buzzing with the wild energy of a Caribbean city centre; the presence of galleries, restaurants and bars, food stands, shops, and many of the most popular accommodation options in the entire city certainly contribute to the positive vibes. This is an area where the arts bursts out of the galleries and onto the city streets in the

most enjoyable ways that a tourist can imagine-- performers rule the streets in colourful costumes, music spills out of the dance halls, painters display their finest works, and galleries host the work of Cuba's finest artists.

If you are not looking to spend much, it might be wise to spend slightly less time in the area, but it certainly should not be missed by anybody missing Havana. It is delightfully photogenic and bound to provide the stuff of memories that are worth every single penny spent in the district.

Enjoying Old Havana: Prado

Next, you should venture to Old Havana's "Prado" neighborhood.

In a bit of a contradiction, this area of Old Havana is not quite as old as the rest of the neighborhood. In fact, Prado is considered to be the "newest" development in all of "Old Havana". So, take that for what it is worth.

Indeed, Prado offers

something that is quite different than the Cathedral surroundings but is nevertheless undeniably compelling. Prado is named after the street that it exists along: Paseo del Prado. Generally, the buildings here are dated from 1900-1950, roughly, rather than other areas of Habana Vieja which are dated back several centuries.

In many ways, Prado acts as the borderline between the borough of Central Havana (Habana Centro) and Old Havana. In many ways, it represents a visual and cultural blend of the old and the new. The roads are developed in a way that allows more cars to travel efficiently, and there are a lot more practical aspects of daily urban life where Prado meets Centro Habana, such as transit stops and more modern markets.

Prado is home to the Bacardi Building, the National Museum of Fine Arts, the Marti Theater, the Grand Theater of Havana, Parque Central ("Central

71

Park"), the Cuban National Ballet, and more popular spots.

The area here is active and alive in an incredible way and it would be odd for you to visit the city without finding yourself in Prado. May as well soak it in while you are there!

Vedado

Although Old Havana was once considered to be the centre of the city, Vedado eventually came along and replaced it.

Technically, Vedado is simply a reward within a

municipality of Plaza de la Revolucion. Vedado is another area that is filled with all sorts of business, just in a different way that Old Havana. Vedado is quite modern and affluent, but it still retains the features that make Havana a beloved city in the hearts of people all around the globe. "La Rampa" is a popular area that marks one border of Vedado, which runs along Calle 23. Vedado also exists along the coastline, and the area on the seawall is Malecon; which is another area that buzzes with the energy of parties and other such social gatherings.

Enjoying Vedado: La Rampa

Technically, La Rampa is a section of Calle 23 (also known as 23 Street). Basically, La Rampa is the portion of the road that connects "L Street" and Malecon. But, in general, La Rampa is best known for being the core of Vedado-- and Vedado is the area that has become the core of the city.

Many tourists choose to stay here in La Rampa rather than areas like Old Havana, which can be very expensive and overwhelming. Although La Rampa is much more modern than the neighborhoods that create Old Havana, La Rampa is often considered to be an "alternative" downtown.

La Rampa is actually hill-like, in a very gradual way. The area slowly moves uphill for the duration of an entire six blocks. In La Rampa, you will find attractions like the Yara Cinema and the Habana Libre Hotel. This is a popular area for wandering, although the presence of six lanes of traffic does provide an entirely different energy and vibe than areas like Calle Obipso in Old Havana; this is not

necessarily a negative change, but certainly is a change in itself.

There is nothing about the area that is not signature Cuban, despite the newer buildings. There are tons of salsa clubs, bars, cinemas, and the live music is encountered just as frequently in this area of the town-- between performances in parks and classic jazz clubs, the diversity is alive and well in this area.

When you are visiting La Rampa, take the chance to grab a famous ice cream from Coppelia if the lineup is not too long-- it is known to sometimes take hours to get your treat from the coolest hot spot for all ages in La Rampa.

Enjoying Vedado: Malecon

By following the natural path of La Rampa, it is very likely that you will end up in Malecon, which is a path in itself that. This seaside section stretches quite a distance of significance within Havana.

Yes, it is true that Malecon is quite far from Old Havana, but it is possible that there isn't a single neighborhood in the city of Havana that so beautifully expresses the heart and soul of the place, as it connects many of the districts to each other. Malecon is not small-- it runs for roughly 8 miles / 5 km along the seawall of Havana. The energy of this area is pretty special.

Cubans and tourists mix in this area in a way that is much different than other regions of the city. The buildings are beautiful. The area brims with Cu-ban culture.

10 of Havana's Most Popular Attractions

In the case that you can't tell by now, Havana is a city that is full of many beautiful people, places, and things.

Havana's history and evolution have provided quite a lot of incredibly interesting sights to behold in the modern day. Today, tourists will often be paralyzed with indecision when they are in the city, as there seems to be all sorts of compelling attractions in every single direction. In an attempt to channel the gifts left behind by the Colonial forces from Spain, the revolutionaries who rose against oppression and implemented socialism in Cuba, and the advancements of the country's modern day. Havana's adventurous story can be told by examining and soaking in many of the remnants of the past that still stand today. Havana is more than just a sunny city by the sea. It is a living piece of all sorts of different histories. The best way to experience Havana is a series of general, leisurely strolls. But, if you are the type of person who likes some direction, here are some landmarks that you should be heading towards. Walk the cobblestone streets that Hemingway fell in love with, have a dance to the rumba music, and feel the sensory splendor that comes from soaking in the salty sea breeze on the Malecon.

Here are a few major points you should not miss:

10. Castillo de los Tres Reyes del Morro

Do yourself a favor while you are in Havana. Do not miss the majesty of Castillo de los Tres Reyes del Morro-- or, as many

tourists and locals have learned to refer to it as, "El Morro". El Morro is a distinct institution in Cuba and has been since it was constructed around the turn of the 16th century into the 17th century. A remnant from a different time, place, and reality, this was more or less a defense structure that was meant to protect the Bay of Havana from the constant threat posed by pirates on the sea. Like so much architecture of the time, El Morro was constructed by an Italian man. Giovanni Battista Antonelli was the architect behind this one. No, it's not needed to protect Havana from the threat of pirates any longer, but it serves a purpose-- specifically for tourists. Although certain features have had to be rebuilt and replicated several times over the years, such as the lighthouse, renovations typically follow the blueprint that was originally put in place by Mr. Antonelli. Although the lighthouse has been rebuilt several times, the lamp inside the house is the same as it has ever been. The area itself is a fortress with lots of distinct structures. Anybody who ventures here and can enjoy the sights of the sea and the rest of Havana; the view of the city from this outlying destination is quite a beautiful thing.

9. Fortaleza de San Carlos de la Cabana

Another classic institution within the Military Park (Parque Historico Militar), this fortress is an impressively sized series of structures located on top of La Cabana hill. Fortaleza de San Carlos de la Cabana was constructed by the Spanish in response to a British occupation; it is a late 18th-century construction. When it was built, there had never been a bigger or more expensive Fort constructed by the Spanish in any of their colonies. The short name for Fortaleza de Sa Carlos de la Cabana is simply "La

Cabana".

The structures that make La Cabana have had many uses through Cuba's storied past. Perhaps most famously, after it had been used as a military prisoner by Batista's government, Che Guevara used it as his HQ after the Castro revolution had succeeded. Now, it is simply a tourist destination, mostly acting as a home to several museums, including a very popular tribute to Che Guevara "Museo de Comandancia del Che", which is a preservation of Che's office. If you visit La Cabana at the right time in the evening, you may witness Ceremonia del Canonazo. This is an interesting display, which includes actors wearing

classical garb and undergo a cannon ceremony.

8. El Capitolio

Many strange rumors circulate around the Capitol building in Havana since it bears a striking resemblance to the equivalent building to this one in Washington D.C... Strangely enough, this is not intended at all, as this 1929 structure was actually inspired by the Pantheon in Paris, France. For many years, this is a building that was mostly functioning as the Cuban Academy of Sciences, but it had been the home of the Cuban government until the Castro's overthrew Batista in 1959. Lately, it has become one of the many homes for Cuba's government once again. Though it may not function as the city's most important government building anymore, this is certainly not from a lack of merit. This is a beautiful feature to the cityscape of Havana and stands out as a massive example of the city's most impressive architecture. There are elements of all sorts of artistic and cultural movements to be found in the detail of El Capitolio, including Neoclassical influences and an undeniably Art Nouveau style. It is one of Cuba's tallest buildings. Since 2013, El Capitolio has been used as a premier parliamentary venue for Cuba's National Assembly. Though its function continues to shift and evolve, this has always been a favourite, jaw-dropping landmark for those who are exploring the city. Due to its impressive height, the dome atop El Capitolio can be spotted from many different parts of Havana.

7. Gran Teatro de La Habana

The Gran Teatro de La Habana, or "The Grand Theatre of Havana", is an awe-inspiring structure. In fact, the building serves as one of the largest opera houses on the entire planet. This Caribbean gem may seem out of place cul-

turally, but it certainly does not look that way. This building, constructed in 1915, manages to be both a majorly distinctive addition to Havana and also something that perfectly melds with the aesthetic of the city. The architect was Paul Belau, a Belgian; the facade was a clearly inspired effort by the baroque influential creation of master Giuseppe Moretti, who applies his inter-nationally acclaimed craft to the project. Whether you attend a performance or not, this is not a sight to skip while you walk the city; if you do attend a performance, however, it is likely not going to be an opera, but a ballet. The Cuba National Ballet currently uses this amazing building as their headquarters. This is a beautiful building, and it is hard to miss too, as it is basically attached to Havana's central park (Parque Central), a location which most curious travelers will naturally gravitate towards.

6. Museo Napoleonico

It is worth checking out the University of Havana. And, when you do, do not miss the Museo Napoleonico. This is an incredible museum featuring some truly remarkable things, including a collection of Julio Lobo's, who is renowned for being one of the most famous Napoleon collectors on the planet; all sorts of totems and memorabilia is featured in this interesting array of Napoleon-themed items. Julio Lobo was a wealthy man who spent many assets on gathering and purchasing all thing that can be legitimately traced to Napoleon Bonaparte. This collection is truly impressive. Lobo sold his collection to the Cuban government in 1959 and now this incredible building is the home of his gatherings.

Body parts such as teeth and hair of Napoleon exist at this palace. There are also weapons, writings, portraits, and more. If you think this is going to be a small collection, think again. There are over 7,000 objects on display; some more interesting than others, naturally.

5. Museo de la Revolucion

Museo de la Revolucion used to be a presidential palace. Now it is a Museum commemorating the famous revolution that created the current socialist system, implemented by the Castro brothers, Che Guevera, and much more. Just like the opera house, Paul Belau designed this building in the early 1900's. A special tribute is given to Che Guevera (the most famous revolutionary, perhaps), and Camilo Cienfuegos (lesser known). Whether you just take a look at the building from the outside or go inside to read and examine, you should not miss the opportunity to

81

take a look at what lurks in the back yard. The yacht that awaits you is not just any old boat, it is the vessel that brought Castro & Co. to Cuba, from Mexico, to begin the takeover of Batista's government.

4. Playas del Este

Playas del Este is not far at all from central Havana. Unlike the other features on this list, Playas del Este is not architecture; it is a little slice of heaven in the form of one of the most popular types of land on the planet... Playas del Este is a beach. Havana can get a little overwhelming. Cuba is full of amazing beaches. Playas del Este just happens to be one of the most incredible beaches in the country, and it is not far from the city centre at all. Of course, there are still all sorts of tourism industry standard facets: restaurants, shops, bars, and more. Different sections of the beach offer different features, though. Santa Maria del Mar is preferred by many tourists looking for something lively. Guanabo is more beloved by locals and tourists who are looking for something slightly less-- well, touristy.

3. Museo Nacional de Bellas Artes

This is one of the best art museums in the entire Caribbean, if not THE best. It is a simply breathtaking of art from around the world-- there is amazing work from Egypt, Greece, Rome, Europe, and of course Cuba. If you have ever enjoyed viewing art before, you will enjoy this gallery. If you have not had the pleasure of experiencing world-class art, this is a great place to start. This is Cuba's most important collection of artistic works and the building itself is a work of art, too. This can be visited during the same day as El Capitolio and Gran Teatro de la Habana, as the three buildings have basically become the most high-profile neighbours in the entire country of Cuba. Tours are available from

professional companies, independent guides, and audio electronic guides as well. If you do not want to hire a guide, you will still have a great time making your way through this giant collection of artistic works, you will likely just be lacking some of the contextual information required to fully appreciate certain elements of the experience.

2. The Colon Cemetery

Cristobal Colon is the name for Christopher Columbus in Cuba. Construction began on this cemetery in 1871, and has been left untouched since the revolution in 1959-- many say that the plot has been "frozen in time" as a matter of mythological fact. In many ways, this is a symbolic visit, and it is quite haunting. Still, despite the fact that it has not been used for over 50 years, it remains Havana's most famous graveyard.

In many ways, it is seen as an "American Graveyard", which helps to explain the fact that it has not been utilized by Cubans since the country took a distinct turn away from

83

American interests.

It was a highly regarded architectural element of Cuban society in the late 19th century and it was named after the man who "Discovered" both Cuba and America, and it is the only "American" graveyard that is named after Columbus (rather ironically using his Spanish name, Cristobal Colon). Colon is reported to have said that Cuba was "the most beautiful island that human eyes have seen."

The architecture takes on more symbolism that political shift in Cuba. There are upside-down torches and winged hourglasses that represent elements of human mortality.

1. Parque Central

Parque Central is beautiful in itself, but its utility in a list like this lies more in the fact that it connects so many interesting sights and attractions to each other. To be honest, it would be impossible to cram everything that

is worth seeing and doing in Havana into just one list! With this in mind, Parque Central is worth wandering, not only because of its own great qualities, but also just the fact that it is the element of the city which physically joins so many different, wonderful parts of Havana.

The park came to fruition in the late 19th century, after Havana's city walls had been destroyed. Many streets of significance such as El Prado, Neptuno, and Zulueta come together here at Parque Central. Many structures that were mentioned on this list, such as the Gran Teatro de La Habana and the Museo de Bellas Artes, can be accessed by a stroll around this wonderful green space.

The park really came together as something beautiful after the 1959 revolution; this was the point in history that saw many of the artistic monuments and greenery included, planted, and installed.

Entertainment Attractions and Activities in Havana

Visit Cigar Shops & Tour The Factories

Do not miss the opportunity to get yourself to one of the best cigar factories in the world-- there are several good options in or very near to Havana.

There are several options in the city, which all have unique benefits, and each now represents one of the best cigar companies in the world; most of the factories carry with them at least one hundred years of history. The Partagas Factory, for example, is 166 years old and has been a beloved tourist destination for some time. Partagas, in particular, is an amazing facility in itself that is no longer used as a factory but still sells cigars. It is a four-story building with the signature style of Cuban

balconies that you might imagine a stereotypical Cuban building having. While you are gawking at the majesty of the factory, do your best to keep yourself from buying the counterfeit cigars being offered to you by locals-- in this case, they are basically certain to be a bad deal. This building was constructed in 1845 and it really looks that way, too.

The factory production at Partagas has moved to another location, but the classic factory is still worth visiting.

When it comes to most local factories, such as the Romeo y Julieta, cigars are still rolled at these factories, and the tours that are given there provide all sorts of interesting information regarding cigar production.

Not to mention, many of these factories include unbelievable deals on world-class cigars, which work as perfect gifts, and are also part of the Cuban tourism experience!

Live Music & Dance

One of the many interesting things about Havana is that amazing live music can happy anywhere, at any time, on any given evening. Sometimes the best music you will hear all night, and the best dancing you will witness, will happen while you are walking from one place to another on the street. Sometimes an amazing player will, by chance, be playing a bar or restaurant that you have ended up at.

However, there are certain clubs and neighborhoods that have great reputations for bringing quality performers in on a substantially consistent basis… This is not to say these clubs, restaurants, and bars will necessarily be "better" than the others, but in our experience, these are great places to start your search for incredible music!

You are unlikely to find a more consistent and diverse music-infused nightclub scene in all of the Caribbean than the one you are sure to encounter in Havana . Prime time always features amazing bands, though cover charge can cost up to $25 to enter in the premium bars meant for tourists. You will not regret it, though. There are also afternoon bands, so the live music is almost constant from 5:00 pm all the way to 2:00 am! There is never a bad band playing anywhere with a following.

Pro tip: You know an inexpensive club is a good club when a lot of Cubans and locals frequent the place.

Another pro tip: There are not very many bad clubs in Havana.

There is a seemingly endless supply of quality salsa, rumba, rap, and jazz music happening in Havana all night, every night.

What are you waiting for? Get out there and shake it!

Getting to Havana

There is an airport in Havana that you can fly to. To get into downtown Havana from the airport is not difficult or expensive, and should not take much longer than 30 minutes.

Taxi. Consider hailing a taxi from in front of the airport. Taxi cabs are highly regarded in terms of safety while traveling in Cuba, and a ride downtown will not cost you more than $25. Try to work the price down to $20 by agreeing on the fare before the ride begins. Taxi drivers in Havana rarely utilize their fare meter, which is a funny quirk you will be sure to notice within your first couple rides.

Charter Bus. Many tour packages will have a chartered bus system that will take you directly to your resort. If you can arrange this, it is easy and smooth, and a very desirable option

Car Rental. Book your car in advance! Once again, in case this is not clear enough, let us repeat this: Cuba is not America!

Cuba is NOT America. There are NOT endless supplies of rental cars for the taking!

Book in advance. Generally, a rental car will cost anywhere from $50-125 a day, with another $15 added for insurance.

Santiago de Cuba

This diverse locale is a true gem of exotic, authentic Caribbean culture

Somehow, Santiago manages to one-up Havana in certain ways. Right when you did not think it would be possible to do so,

Santiago somehow concentrates culture in a way that creates an opposing city that surely bears as many differences as it does similarities to Havana.

Santiago de Cuba is geographically quite far from Havana, in the context of Cuba and the Caribbean at least. They are at complete opposite ends of the island... In fact, Santiago is nearer to different countries, such as the Dominican Republic and Haiti, than it is in vicinity to the capital of Cuba… This makes a difference in all sorts of ways, direct and indirect.

Santiago has a freeing, rebellious energy that creates a vibe that flows with liberation and freedom of spirit. The Afro-Caribbean influence in Cuba is significantly closer to the source in Santiago, and this may be the reason that this energy permeates the rest of the nation with such a vivacious strength.

Santiago is wild in its energy. Its beauty is not peaceful but busy. The history of Santiago is one of all sorts of rebellion and uprising. The impact of the shadows of the Castro rebellion, the Diego Valazquez de Cuellar influence, the Bacardi rum empire, and the birth of Cuban music as a whole: it all stems from the active, lively streets of Santiago del Cuba. In Santiago, you can feel the rhythm of this history; it is tangible and crisp.

Yes, Santiago is less like Havana than it is like a more authentic, Un-American New Orleans. The roots of Spanish colonialism act as a supportive foundation for all of the subversive power that worked to turn such forces upside down.

Santiago de Cuba is the second biggest, second most populated city in the country. Whether it is the second best or whether it displaces Havana is a matter of debate and, ultimately, personal opinion.

" Santiago is wild in its energy - its beauty is not peaceful but busy

Casco Historico

The "Old Town" of Santiago de Cuba not a UNESCO World Heritage Site like Havana, but it is preserved as a National Monument instead. It has had this distinction since 1978. This neighborhood within the city is defined by an era-based city limit: the city at the end of the 19th century is the borderline here. The preservation efforts are mostly focused on the Spanish colonial architecture, but also feature corresponding to Cuba's move away from colonial forces and towards becoming its own Republic.

Enjoying Casco Historico: Parque Cespedes

If you are a person who enjoys people-watching, there is nowhere better than the heart of this district; specifically, Parque Cespedes is where you will want to be. The area is full of eccentrics and eccentricities. Cespedes is great for the urbanite and the outdoorsman.

This has recently become famous as an area with an open Wi-Fi signal, which may be metaphorically more meaningful than it is in a literal sense.

Parque Cespedes is everything that this city represents: a hustling stampede of love, life, creativity, and infectious energy. It's a beautiful park in the middle of the historical district of the town of Santiago de Cuba. The surrounding architec-ture is somehow perfect, even though the original meaning of the colonial structures has had its meaning changed by the modern context: somehow, it all makes sense. The statue of the namesake of the park, Carlos Manuel de Cespedes, the man who put fuel on the fire to begin the conquest toward Cuban independence way back in 1868 resides in this park, which is somehow the perfect symbol for this city: and, more specifically, the perfect symbol for this area of this city.

The streets that create the border for the park at the iconic San Pedro, Santo Tomas, Heredia, and Aguilera. Surrounding Parque Cespedes are many of the iconic historical structures that have evolved into most of the city's primary tourist attractions: Diego Valazquez's home, the San Carlos Club, the Casa Granda Hotel, and even the town hall, among other interesting and important business and institutions of past and present.

10 of
Santiago de
Cuba's Most

Popular Attractions

Santiago de Cuba is an incredible example of a Caribbean city. Although it is not as large or populated as Havana, it does not lack in authenticity, creativity, or spirit. Yes, it is the second largest city in Cuba, but the history and culture are arguably the most vibrant in the entire country... Santiago is considered to be the birthplace and the inspiration for the Cuban Revolution, which the city continues to pay tribute to in many different ways, including public monuments, names of streets and landmarks, and historical museums that are dedicated to certain elements of the revolution. Santiago has continued to evolve within this revolutionary, liberation-based archetype, and the buildings represent this growth, as does the energy of the city itself. The city is young, fun, and full of the finer things in life-- historic colonial structures are made amazing to look at and explore because their imperial power has been stripped from them-- the tools of previous oppression become symbols of freedom in this way: Cuba Libre! (in every sense of the term).

Santiago de Cuba is, in many ways, a perfect example of an Afro-Caribbean culture that is fully embraced by an entire city. This vibe digs deeply into the expressions of the city and they can be witnessed by paying attention to the art-- both performance and visual; the dancing, music styles, art that fills the galleries, and city sculptures are all proficient in furthering this motif.

The vibrancy of the last 500 years on this part of the island has led to progression, regression, destruction, celebration, and nearly everything in between. Many of the most popular sights and attractions in Santiago de Cuba tell this story in one way or another.

10. Museum of the Clandestine Struggle

There are a lot of re-imagined buildings in cities like this, where great revolutions have taken places. A fine example of this is the Museum of the Clandestine Struggle (also known as Museo de la Lucha Clandestina) which is now a big yellow building,but was once the home of the police who enforced the previous system. The "Clandestine Struggle" is an era of the revolution, and a factor that contributed toward revolt, that is certainly worth documenting. These museums teach us that the revolution took a lot more than Che Guevera and the Castro brothers-- this museum, specifically, focuses on the contributions to the revolution that were made by a man named Frank Pais, who stood up to the Batista government in his own way. Perhaps ironi-

95

cally, Frank Pais and his crew of uprising residents set fire to the very buildings that the museum is now housed within during the height of the political intensity between the people and their government. Now, the effects of the fire need to be pointed out to be seen, you would never know it would have happened-- the building is quite a treat for the eyes. It is a beautiful structure with a fine courtyard that provides a beautiful perspective over the city of Santiago de Cuba.

9. Casa de Diego Velazquez (Museo de Ambiente Historico Cubano)

Representing another era of Cuban history, the Casa de Diego Velazquez can be found on your stroll through Parque Cespedes and certainly cannot be missed. The Cubans will generally refer to the presence of the Spanish in the late 15th and early 16th century as the first truly damaging colonial trauma on their culture.

By acknowledging that this chapter is over, we acknowledge the absence of previous oppression, which creates a sense of freedom. So, some artifacts remain, such as the previous residence of the Conquistador and Governor of Diego Velazquez, which is now being used as the Museo de Ambiente Historico Cubano. Objectively, it is a beautiful structure in many ways, and it has a lot of different uses and dimensions. Although the upstairs of the building was the home of Velazquez, there was a gold foundry in the basement, and that intense, ancient foundry furnace still stands in the basement. The level of luxury from so many centuries ago provides an immersive experience that will give any visitor an impression of how the Spanish empire carried itself during the days of its height... Restoration efforts on the Velazquez home began in 1965. The museum tells

96

the stories of the colonial Spanish presence in Cuba from the 1500s to the 1800s and does a comprehensive job in doing so, with many different rooms showing many different phases during this relatively large window of time. Viewed objectively, there is a lot of beauty to be found here, with stained glass, porcelain, and a treasury of antiques. Many English speakers will offer tours of the building, which can be recommended if you are interested in understanding the cultural context, rather than just treating your eyes to the splendors of the contents that are on display in the museum.

8. Jardin Botanico

Not technically within the city of Santiago de Cuba, the Jardin Botanico is still worth mentioning due to the close proximity especially. It is about a 15-minute drive from the city, and it is quite a sight to behold indeed. Jardin Botanico as actually a UNESCO Biosphere Reserve; a protect-ed environment of mountains, forests, and beautiful beaches. Literally, the area is known as the "Garden of the Ferns." There are more than 3000 plants in this area, which is full of at least 228 native plants and just under 70 exotic plants that have been introduced. The ferns themselves are wonderful, but so is everything else, including a massive set of stairs that climbs over 1,000 metres and finds the top of the Gran Piedra peak, providing a spectacular view of the region.

7. Castillo de San Pedro del Morro

Another UNESCO protected piece of infrastructure, this a world-class World Heritage Site that is quite similar in some ways to Castillo de los Trey Reyes del Morro in Havana… However, some will say that this fortress has been preserved even better. In fact, San Pedro del Morro is considered by some to have succeeded the most in its preservation

97

out of all Spanish fortresses that were constructed
in the 1600s. Although
Antonelli designed this in
1587, it took over 40 years
for construction to get un-
derway and for this hill-top
structure to begin taking
shop.

Much like Castillo de
los Trey Reyes del Mor-
ro in Havana, this was
a fortress to present an
important settlement from
the threat of pirates. It
also acted as a jail in the
18th century, briefly, and
then became a fortress for
defense once again.

The museum within the
fortress walls today tells
the story of the pirates, the
Navy, and provides more
general historical context
about Santiago de Cuba's
development through the
ages. Again, like Castil-
lo de los Trey Reyes del
Morro in Havana, there is
a canon firing at sundown
that is absolutely not worth
missing. It should also not
going without saying that
this is a beautiful spot to
catch the sunset from.

6. Cementerio de Santa Ifigenia

It is worth checking out
the Cementerio de San-
ta Ifigenia, even though
a graveyard may not fit
your initial impression as a
great space to visit on your
tourist trip... This cem-
etery, however, is much
different than the deserted
Colon cemetery in Hava-
na-- in many ways, it is
the opposite. Rather than
becoming deserted and
forgotten, this is a place
where many of the heroes
from Cuban political and
social culture have been
buried; respect continues
to be given to them on a
regular basis. Many tombs
act as grand monuments,
such as the Mausoleum
of Jose Marti. This is an
aesthetically gorgeous
mausoleum that is much
taller and more significant
looking than any other
structure in the cemetery,
and is a beautiful place to
explore, specifically when
light breaks in during the
morning hours.

Graves and tombs for

Carlos Manuel de Cespedes, Frank Pais, and Emilio Bacardi can also be found at the Cementerio de Santa Ifigenia. Many significant Cuban citizens and cultural figures end up being buried here, including Fidel Castro after his death in 2016. Indeed, visiting this cemetery and the one in Havana can be an interesting discovery in the contrast of how this society views their dead. This is another place that it can be a very good idea to hire an English speaking guide, as there are so many important figures with rich stories that provide meaning to the experience.

5. Bacardi Rum Factory (and Emilio Bacardi's Museum)

Yes, the swanky, fashionable new HQ for Bacardi is located way over in Bermuda, but would you be surprised to learn that the original factory is right here in Santiago de Cuba? Born from the booming bustle of this Caribbean town, Bacardi has become something of a cultural symbol in this city of Santiago. This factory opened way back in 1868, and there is a lot of amazing information about the company and about rum in general. The factory owners had to leave during the revolution, but rum production continued after their departure by state-run rum brands that produced other domestic rums. There are no tours in the factory, but there is a small rum bar, and you can buy souvenirs.

4. Cuartel Moncado (Museo Historico 26 de Julio)

The 26th of July is a massive date for Cuba's revolution. This is the day that the rebels commanded by the Castro brothers and Che Guevera made a massive attempt to seize weapons from this very site, which is now a museum dedicated to their efforts. This was early in the revolution, however, on the 26th of July 1953. The rebels struggled for years after this, and their attempt on July 26th was not necessarily a successful one in the immediate sense. However, it was not a failure either, as the revolutionary squad significantly improved their legitimacy and profile; this was a massive momentum shift that put the odds in their favor more than they had been previously. Many historians and revolution buffs commemorate this date, marking it as the beginning of the Cuban revolution. The museum is dedicated to this, and the venue could not be any better. There are still bullet holes in the walls and other evidence of the revolutionary attacks. The museum is full of great artifacts and information regarding Che Guevara, Fidel Castro, Raul Castro, and more-- much more, as the museum's historical reach actually begins the story with Cuba's original colonial struggles in the 16th century. However, the museum takes the direction of focusing squarely on the revolutionary struggle that the rebels took to overthrow the Batista regime in the 1950s, with first-hand personalized dedications and commemorations to the effort that the brave revolutionaries took on July 26.

This is considered by many to be the most important and distinct museum that the tourist can possibly make their way to while in Santiago de Cuba-- do not miss your chance to check this one out!

3. Vista Alegre

In the 1920s and 1930s, Vista Alegre was the upscale side of town. Back when there were far more distinct class differences in Cuban society, Vista Alegre represented sophistication in the form of neoclassical mansions and other luxurious residences. Since becoming socialist and taking great measures to create equality within the country, these mansions have been repurposed by the state and are not utilized as public re-

100

sources such as schools, restaurants, and several types of state-run offices. It simply was not fair to have some Cubans living in the luxurious mansions of Vista Alegre.

Although simply wandering through this area provides appeal for most tourists, there is a lot of great stuff to check out here, too. Centro Cultural Africano Fernando Ortiz is a popular attraction for tourists, which is a museum that features a collection of artifacts and crafts from Africa-- the African culture in Cuba is particularly alive in Santiago de Cuba, so it is worth checking this out to broaden your understanding of the cultural mosaic that the city creates.

Casa del Caribe is in Vista Alegre, too, as well as the Museo de Imagen.

2. Museo Provincial Bacardi Moreau

If you are looking for something more structured, head over to the museum that was built by Carlos Segrera in conjunction with Emilio Bacardi Moreau. This is one of the first museums that came to being in Cuba, and it is interesting in ways that relate to a lot more than just the famous rum that many people will associate with the term "Bacardi"-- this is a huge collection of all things Cuba that was constructed in 1927 and still remains very relevant today. Art collected here tells the story of intense Spanish conquest, the struggle for Cuban independence, and more.

This museum has its home in a 1929 neoclassical style building. The Museo Provincial Bacardi Moreau has collectibles and art from all over the planet, though there is certainly a focus on pieces that have some kind of connection to the Cuban culture that can be seen directly or through external influence on the life that we witness on the streets of Santiago. One of Bacardi Moreau's most interest-

101

ing pieces is something he traveled to Egypt to find in 1912: a real mummy.

1. Plaza de la Revolucion

Located just slightly to the North East of the city centre, you will have to make your way to this iconic plaza within the city of Santiago de Cuba. This is a famous site for a lot of reasons. Important events just keep happening here, which is what brings more and more renown to the site. Obviously, it is another site which commemorates the people's revolution in Cuba, but it is also more than that. This is a place where Fidel Castro delivered some of his most impactful and powerful speeches. The Pope has spent time here in celebration as well. In general, it is a site where people come to protest and has been a bastion of liberal thought and freedom in Cuba for decades. There is also a very impressive monument: General Antonio Maceo, who is another hero of the people, is depicted on horseback except he is surrounded by weaponry such as saw-toothed machetes which arise from the ground around him. This powerful sculpture was erected in this location in 1991, with the presence of Fidel Castro attending.

This is a place that is designated for meaningful political moments and continues to be filled with them, adding to the mythology and symbolism of the area. Don't forget to check out the Museo Holografia in the park, which is an underground, indoor area that features popular holographic images that show representations of key moments of revolution, revolts, and the struggle for liberty from

Santiago offers what seem to be infinite amounts of talented salsa musicians

General Maceo and more.

Entertainment Attractions and Activities in Santiago de Cuba

Live Music: Casa de las Traiciones & More

Whether you are looking to listen to some amazing live music or actually get moving and dance, this place manages to be extremely accalimed and popular, but still keep its authentic feel; Casa de las Traiciones is a true music club of Santiago. It has a loose, genuine, and underground feel, despite the fact that it has become one of the most reputable places to have a good time in the entire country. Don't miss this one!

Casa de las Traciones is tucked away and nearly hidden in the beautiful little Tivoli district, but there is nothing quaint about what happens here. The musicians, of many different types, will play top notch music, whether it is improvised or structured. The energy is incomparable and they will rarely bring in a performer who is not going to bring down the house.

This bar features professional artwork, great drinks, world-class music, and the gritty, underground hope that you may be looking for. It is a ture Afro-Cuban classic.

Keep your eyes peeled for the following places: Santiago Cafe, Tropicana Santiago, and more-- but also keep your ears open to any attractive rhythyms, and follow them!

Much like Havana, Santiago offers what seem to be infinite amounts of talented salsa, rumba, rap, and jazz musicians doing their thing in the city. There is always-- ALWAYS-- something going on in a place like this-- a city which blends calm with wild energy.

Saturday Nights: Noche Santiaguera

A weekly outdoor party in the city-- what could be better? Noche Santiaguera features amazing musicians, food vendors, and a large crowd of locals and tourists gathering to enjoy the pleasures together... Good cities know how to party, and this is one of the best unifying events in the Caribbean-- and it occurs weekly! Meet the locals and have fun!

Guided Exploration: Walking Tours

Santiago de Cuba is a city we would be more likely to recommend a walking tour in than Havana. It is smaller and the significant buildings are more frequent and more concentrated. There are private tours and group tours that take you through many of the attractions we have laid out in our top 10 list, as well as much more, such as the home of a young Fidel Castro and more. If there is one city in Cuba to traverse on foot, it would be Santiago. The guides are often top notch, exemplifying the greatness of Cuban people.

Check out the 'Heroic City' on foot and see all of the locations that contrib-uted to the oppression and liberation of the people of Santiago de Cuba. Symbols of independence are everywhere-- otherwise ordinary locations that had some direct or indirect like to the revolutionaries who fought for Cuba's independence are waiting to be discovered and many guides know the city inside and out. More than this, a walking tour can help you grow familiar with the "little things" that make a place distinct and have an impact on the way citizens of a location choose to, and are pressured to, exist by their natural, social, and political environments.

Santiago de Cuba is also nice to walk because it is exotic, colourful, full of hills, and highly concentrated with significant landmarks. Many tours will take you through Loma de San Juan, Moncada Barracks, and many of the spots we have already mentioned in this guide like Castillo El Morro, the cemetery, and Park Cespedes.

Getting to Santiago de Cuba

There is an airport that has fairly frequent charter flights arriving in Santiago de Cuba. It is not as major of an airport as the one in Havana, but a connecting flight between the two airports is typically around $100. This is the most common way to arrive, though you can also show up by bus; a bus ticket from Havana to Santiago de Cuba is about $50, and the distance between the two cities is roughly 860 km.

Getting to the city from the airport:

Taxi. Many people choose to hire a taxi since the airport is only about a 20-minute drive from the core of the city and will not cost more than $10 USD. This is a popular choice.

Charter Bus. Many tour packages will have a chartered bus system that will take you directly to your resort or the hotel specified within your tour package. If you can arrange this, it is easy and smooth, and a very desirable option.

Car Rental. Car rental rates are similar to that in Havana. Affordable but not "cheap".

The Province of Matanzas

Matanzas is the second largest province in all of Cuba. In general, there are two major locations in Matanzas that interest tourists. Ironically, these two places are among the most distinctly different from each other in terms of what type of tourists they attract and what they offer to a tourist. These locations are the capital city of the province (the city of Matanzas), and the iconic resort town of Varadero. The environmental diversity is huge.

106

The distinctions and contradictions within the province run deep. In some areas, the vast nature of Matanzas is among the most beautiful and perfectly kept in the entire nation. In others, we see that Matanzas is heavily industrialized, with mills, tankers, refineries, and petroleum wells open to be spotted, scattered around the province.

On the southern coast of the province, there are some amazing sights to behold: Cienaga de Zapata is a giant marsh that constitutes Cuba's largest wetland. Near here, to the East of the peninsula, is the location of the famous historical Bay of Pigs invasion. Up north and to the west, the terrain is noticeably rocky, with a few distant islands located off of the coast which is lined with mangroves. There are some popular beaches in

> **Cienaga de Zapata is a giant marsh that constitutes Cuba's largest wetland**

this area, too.

In terms of cities, Matanzas is the capital and Varadero (a resort town more than a 'city') is the most frequently visited--but Cardenas, Colon, and Jovellanos are also notable urban locales. None will disappoint, but these cities don't quite stack up to the others.

The City of Matanzas

If you think it is time for a change of pace, from the wild cities of irreverent fun and effervescent hedonism represented by Havana and Santiago de Cuba, Matanzas may be what you are looking

107

for. Nothing about Cuba seems particularly modern, but all of Matanzas has something that is somehow more rustic and mysterious than many other areas of the country… It is like a treasure chest in the woods that has been gathering moss for a slightly suspicious amount of time, untouched. Luckily, you are free to touch it.

In fact, the City of Matanzas is often tragically overlooked by tourists and travelers. Sometimes literally, as people on their way to Varadero do not even realize that they are passing through this subtle gem… Those who do make an effort to invest some of their time in Matanzas will surely be patting themselves on the back for the decision that they have made to stop by. It is a distinct and wonderful place that is quite unique in relation to the limited sample size of Cuban and Caribbean settlements.

The city of the Matanzas is a mecca of traditional Cuban arts; much of the mythical poetry and story that pervades Cuban culture was born and nurtured in Matanzas, even though does not always get the credit. For a long stretch during the 1700s and 1800s, there was more recognition of this fact and Matanzas was treated with more reverence. Now, this has been forgotten about ever-so-slightly, largely due to the attraction that is so strongly felt by tourists towards the "Big 3" of Havana, Santiago de Cuba, and Varadero. In this guide we have included Matanzas before Varadero due to cultural significance, not necessarily due to favoritism, and definitely not in an acknowledgment of their relative popularity in comparison to each other. Those who know Matanzas, appreciate it.

There is just "something" about Matanzas that has

always led to the breeding of fantastic poets, musicians, writers, dancers, and artists of all kinds. It is hard to understand exactly "why" this is the case, but the results speak for themselves.

Rumba was born in Matanzas, too; rumba is so strongly felt all throughout Cuba and most commonly associated with other cities, but the source is right here in modest Matanzas. Matanzas also acted as a nest that hatched several African spiritual and religious streams of thought. Due to the immense amount of culture, Matanzas supports this with an incredibly fine theatre.

Step into Matanzas. The charms may not be as obvious as other Cuban locales, but it is absolutely a valid opinion to state that the culture may actually be richer.

10 of the City of Matanzas' Most Popular Attractions

For some, Matanzas is literally just a town that is passed on the trip between Havana and Varadero. For others, Matanzas is literally the most precious and meaningful city that they encounter in Cuba. Yes, for those who appreciate the more subtle and nuanced things in life, and who do not need to be sucked up in wild energy of the urban-Caribbean, Matanzas is a dream. Matanzas is the capital city of the province with the same name. It is generally regarded as an industrial city, but does not give the same feeling

109

that many "industrial city" settings in the Western World give off. Roughly 120,000 people live in the city of Matanzas-- not a huge amount, but the city still has quite a buzzing energy.

One of the strangest

colonialists coming over and wiping out the local population of Cuban natives who lived on the land before they had arrived. Others will say the name actually has more to do with the mass murder of animals and livestock that were shipped in during the early days.

Matanzas today remains geared towards authentic culture and creativity and is less concerned with being a "big city" than the others the come before in this guide. It was well known as being the "Athens of Cuba" or "Cuban Venice" once upon a time. Today, this claim does not stand the test of time, but it could be considered as being the "Athens" in a sense of mythology and culture, rather than in terms of urban activity. It is sleepy like Venice, and that comparison holds water a little better, as cities like Havana compare to Rome in a similar way. The buildings gener-

things about Matanzas is that the word translates directly to "mass murder" in Spanish, which is likely a reference to the Spanish

ally feature neoclassical design elements and the city certainly began to feel a period of serious evolution toward the end of the 1700s. Like many other important areas of Cuba, Matanzas is protected by seaside fortresses that have adapted their utility for the purpose of becoming tourist destinations.

10. The Bridges

Matanzas is known as the City of Bridges and for good reason. There are typically around 20 functional bridges in the city, serving a practical purpose, but also are representative of a unique architectural and aspect level of the city's architecture blending with the past and present of Matanza. There are 17 bridges that, at different points of the city, act as functional ways to cross the three different rivers that run through Matanzas. This is likely another reason why Matanzas is known by many as being the "Venice of Cuba", just as it was called

the "Athens of Cuba" for its seemingly unique ability to churn out a high percentage of Cuba's most vital poets. The Canimar bridge is one of the most beautiful in the city, crossing the Canimar river in a truly picturesque fashion. If you were to ask us, we would suggest, if you had to spend a bit of time at one particular bridge for whatever reason, that you head toward Puente Calixto Garcia-- also known as Calixto Garcia Bridge. This is a really beautiful structuring that runs over the Rio San Juan, a river that is much beloved by those who leisurely use kayaks. The bridges, for the most part, will connect you from one attraction toward another, and the Calixto Garcia bridge is no different. Nearby are some of the most exciting attractions in all of Matanzas. For lovers of architecture, trying to spot every bridge in town is a bit of a fun and rewarding challenge. For others who are more casual about their appreciation of architecture, the random encounters with the bridges should still supply a bit of a subtle delight. Including the next on this list.

9. Plaza de la Vigia

Plaza de la Vigia is just a stone's throw away from the iconic Puente Calixto Garcia in Matanzas. The literal translation of this is "Lookout Place", and Matanzas is not unique in having had to have kept a consistent lookout for some time. To be clear, the plaza itself was not a lookout point, but it was located close to the old fort which was built to defend the area from the constant threat of being attacked by pirates, which, again, is a typical story for Cuban settlements. However, this plaza is quite a unique one in terms of Cuba. It is not large, but it is a throughline that will lead any travelling wanderer to a lot of key destinations and attractions around the city. It is a flashy, attractive plaza that burst with life and colour. In a historical and a current context, Plaza de la Vigia is the cultural (and literal) foundation of the city of Matanzas; it all moves outward from there.

Matanzas was founded in 1693. Plaza de la Vigia was the first town square in the city. Moving out from the plaza, the rest of the city was gradually developed.

Unlike other cities though, the Matanzas decided to deconstruct and destroy their fort when it lost any purpose or relevance in the 1850s. The city took the opportunity to build some aesthetically pleasing buildings in the place of that fortress, which is something that very few cities in Cuba have done, and has contributed to the interesting and unique 'vibe' of Cuba's Athens.

Buildings such as the Aduana building, which is now the Provincial Court of Matanzas, the fire station, the Junco Palace, and even the Sauto Theater are connected by Plaza de la Vigia.

We recommend that you access Plaza de la Vigia via the Calixto Garcia Bridge. The view of the city's flourishing colours, centralized within this important city square. Today, Plaza de la Vigia remains as the city's busiest and most vital cultural hub, which makes it a very important place for all sorts of activities, whether they are leisurely, cultural, or political-- if it's happening in Matanzas and it is important, it is likely connected to the historic and ever relevant Plaza de le Vigia.

8. Parque Libertad

It is not a long journey between the first few items on the list. One can cross the Calixto Garcia Bridge, enjoy some time in Plaza de la Vigia, and then saunter on their way over to Parque Libertad. Parque Libertad, of course, translates quite clearly to "liberty park" and the area is quite freeing in its energy. Parque Libertad is home to some true Matanzas gems, including Cuba's own statue of liberty. However, Matanzas' "liberty statue" is much different than the one found just off the coast of New York City. This statue is powerful; the represented image is a woman standing with open arms and wrists that hold the remnants of chains that have been broke. She woman shouts "Freedom!" There is also a statue made from bronze that depicts the image of the classic Cuban freedom symbol Jose Marti, who was a famous Cuban poet and also the founder of the Cuban Revolutionary Party.

Many strolls through the city end up in this park, which provides a brilliant addition to any tourist's day spent in Matanzas. In the immediate vicinity of this wonderful space are significant buildings such as Velasco Theater, Hotel Velasco, the Museo Farmacaceutico, the Spanish Casino, and some government buildings.

Although you should end up here by chance with any standard stroll through the city, try to ensure that you do not allow yourself to miss it.

7.Palacio de Gobierno

One imposing structure will stick out while wandering about Parque Libertad; Palacio de Gobierno. This aesthetically impressive structure was constructed in 1853. The stylistic design elements are basically second to none. There are giant arches that form a beautiful walkway, which is almost entirely covered. The image of this side of the structure is visible from Parque Libertad and, generally, it is an image that would be impossible to miss; this is one of the most visually distinct and prominent structures in all of Matanzas.

Today, this palace is used as a government building, and is currently the home of the Popular Power; this is the local government. Literally,

the term "Palacio de Gobierno" translates to the "Governor's Palace." Although it is still used for government, one assumes that the power that is held within this palace is less intense than it had been in when the building was originally designed and constructed in the 19th century. Now, it simply contributes to the light, beautiful feel of the core of Matanzas.

6. Palacio de Justicia

The Palacio de Justicia is surrounded by some of the most beautiful buildings in Matanzas. In the area of Plaza de la Vigia, all of the architectural delights are in elite company with each other, forming a formidable combination of high-status neighbours in terms of the cultural and political significance of the buildings. The Palacio de Justicia is not necessarily lesser than any of its local companions, though it is just a single example that exists among quite a collection of pronounced structures.

Palacio de Justicia was constructed in 1826 and then rebuilt nearly one hundred years later. A century after it was erected, it was remodeled and rebuilt in 1911. To this day, restoration generally continues on the building, which translates literally to "Palace of Justice."

This Palace of Justice has been a staple feature of the city of Matanzas for a sizeable amount of the city's rich past. The palace represents a welcome presence of neoclassical architecture in the city. Not only this, but the Palacio de Justicia is actually the first neoclassical building that was ever erected in Cuba. Currently, the building is used to house some of the city's municipal government operations.

5. Che Mural

When many Westerners and travellers think of the revolutionary struggle that occurred in Cuba, the first face that comes to mind is that of Che Guevara. Che Guevara was an iconic figure for the revolution, but many are surprised to learn that he was not even a Cuban native. Che had traveled around South America and grew disenchanted and outraged with what we considered to be the disgraceful, tragic impact of American imperialism. He met the Castro brothers, Raul and Fidel, in Mexico, as they plotted their potential overthrow of the American-backed Batista regime. Che Guevara was instrumental in turning this dream into a reality, and he continued to share his findings and socialist strategies with governments all around the world with a charming demeanor that was able to win over people around the globe-- and the marked him as a serious threat to American and general imperialist interests. Eventually, Che was assassinated for his efforts, as he assumed he would be. Che Guevara remains an extremely popular symbol around the

globe, but his contributions are especially appreciated in Cuba.

Here in Matanzas, appreciation is shown in one specific way that really stands out: a mural of Che Guevara. The image of Che is quite an iconic one: it is his headshot... A simple shot of his face, complete with long hair, and his red star cap. However, the mural has one specific element that makes it truly unique: it was built with stones. This mosaic is one of the most famous images of Che within Cuba and it is certainly worth taking a look at.

4. Teatro Sauto

Not only is Teatro Sauto (the Sauto Theatre) considered to be one of the most beautiful buildings in all of Matanzas, but this is generally revered as being the most beautiful theatre in all of Cuba. The Sauto Theater began its operations in 1863 after

117

an extended period of construction. Since then, Teatro Sauto's external appearance has served as an incredible symbol for the city of Matanzas-- a city which is very well known for being a bastion of folk and professional art, as well as creativity. The theatre is not a small arena for performance, that is for sure: the theatre's seating area is U-shaped and it seats as many as 775 people. The theatre is covered with top-of-the-line, state-of-the-art wood-panelling that creates an amazing aesthetic within the building. The curtain is also famous at this theatre, as it often features its own painting, and becomes a work of art in itself. This is a metaphor of the level of artistic detail that goes into every detail of this theatre space, and it is also just a contributing to the reputation that Teatro Sauto holds as for being one of the most incredible theatres in the entire country of Cuba-- a country that does not treat its architecture lightly, especially when it comes to its professional art performance houses.

3. Bellamar Caves

The Bellamar Caves, or "Cuevas de Bellamar" as they are called by the locals, are impressive and even a little bit scary. They are underground and do not exactly scream out as being an ideal version of a "tropical tourist destination" but if you are in Matanzas you should absolutely take the little trip out of town to this creepy, cool caves. There is something about this destination that is truly magical, showing the majesty of nature in a way that we do not always get to see, and in a way that one would not expect to encounter during their sweet, sunny, and tropical vacation to the island haven of Cuba. However, once you enter these caves, it is impossible not to be impressed by the wild, jagged stalactites and stalagmites that reach

out from the roof and walls of the rocky caverns. Also on the walls are a lot of ancient images that were written on the walls by the indigenous locals. The ancient natives had clearly found some value in transcribing images of rivers and streams on the walls and it is truly a mind-expanding sight to behold. The caves have traces of life in them, and traces of biological evolution, that make scientists believe that they are at least 300,000 years old!

2. Castillo de San Severino

This is a true castle in the Spanish sense. It was built in the first half of the 18th century, in 1735 to be exact. Like many of the strong fortresses scattered around the country of Cuba, there was one

119

very practical purpose when this infrastructure was originally constructed. The British used to punish this particular fort of the Spanish during the colonial battles, as Cuba was a highly prioritized asset that was constantly being sought after by all of the Western imperial powers. This particular castle was bombarded extensively in 1762 and was not rebuilt until the 1770s. At that point, Castillo de San Severino assumed the role of being an offloading point for slaves. Slavery is one of the aspects of colonialism in the previously dominant Spanish-Cuban society that locals are most upset about, in many cases. It is also where the strong African influence of the Afro-Cuban arts and culture come from. The current purpose of the structure, Museo de la Ruta de los Exclavos, San Severino became a prison for some time. Now, the castle-like museum is

a tourist destination that offers a pleasant view over the Bahia de Matanzas.

1. Iglesia de Monserrate

Once you have explored the city streets to a satisfactory level, it will be time to make your way up to Iglesia de Monserrate. This is a picturesque church that is stationed in such a way that it looks down on the city from a high perspective, and it is quite a climb to make your way up to this wonderful feature. The church itself is surely beautiful, but the view of the always verdant and green, growing, and luscious Matanzas is what makes the experience a truly remarkable one that must not be missed by anyone capable of making the journey up. Take a gander at the deep greens of the Valle de Yumuri on one side, and the vibrant city of Matanzas on the other. The climb is a reasonable 1.5 kilometres and promises to be an incredibly rewarding trek. The Spanish colonial forces may have built this church in this location to assert social status, but now the view is to be shared among all who are interested in the beauty of the Matanzas city and province. Make your way to the lookout, where you can obviously gain some perspective on the area, but also eat good ranchon-style food, listen to some iconic Cuban music, and enjoy a beverage or two. Generally speaking, it is recommended that tourists begin their day by visiting Iglesia de Monserrate in the earlier hours of the morning.

Cultural Experiences, Entertainment, and Activities in Matanzas

Live Performances

There may not be as consistently fulfilling programming in Matanzas as there is Havana and Santiago de Cuba, but that is not to say that there will not be some incredible performances occurring. The first thing you should

122

check is the performance schedule at Teatro Sauto; all sorts of national-level music and dance will find its way into this sacred Cuban venue and the standard of quality and calibre brought by the professional performances here is absolutely second to none.

Keep your eyes peeled for the Sala de Conciertos Jose White, too. This is a beautifully restored building from the 1870s that often hosts symphonies and other forms of classical music. This may not be your ideal, imagined view of a Cuban music experience, but it is what it is, and that certainly is not a bad thing.

If you think that you might have any type of interest in Cuban rumba

123

dance you should absolutely seize the opportunity to enjoy the form in the city that it was born in: of course, we speaking of Matanzas. Matanzas was the birthplace of rumba dancing and despite the fact that the rumba "scene" may not be as busy and hot as it is in cities like Havana and Santiago but the authenticity here in Matanzas is second to none; indeed, if rumba music is one of the reasons you have decided to choose Cuba as the tourist destination that you will visit, you must include Matanzas on your list of places to visit whilst in the country.

Personal Exploration: Walking The City

Matanzas is the type of city that is perfect for a walking tour of some kind; whether it is in a group, personal, or with some kind of audio or written guide. So much of the city is centralized near the main plaza and everything that is not includes a beautiful walk through the folksy streets which have been walked by the journeyed feet of so many famous Cuban poets, providing inspiration that has allowed the residual impact of Matanzas' magic to permeate the borders of the province and echo throughout the entire country.

A walking tour is a remarkably efficient expedition that will provide information that amplifies the meaning of so many monuments and features, providing context that will help you understand the country's identity through becoming more intimate with the whimsical stories carried within the city streets. Find yourself a local who knows the ins and the outs of the area and allow yourself to get excited about everything that Matanzas has to offer that just can't be seen on the surface.

There are all sorts of fun ways to approach walking through the city, such as making an attempt to spot every bridge in town-- the city is not very geographically imposing, as it is only home to roughly 140,000 Cubans...

History of The City of Matanzas

1690 is the first year of direct significance to consider when looking into the history of Matanzas, as it is the year that a royal decree was issued that declared Matanzas to be a settlement for a small group of families from the Canary Islands. Although, obviously, previous events were key in shaping the forces that created Matanzas, the city was founded in the year 1693. Soon after it was originally founded, development of sugar plantations was initiated and Matanzas was a central port during the intense Spanish colonialism that Cuba suffered through the later 18th and 19th centuries; this had a huge impact on the population of Matanzas, as the percentage of the town's population that were slaves ranges from 30% to 65% in those years. The revolutionary spirit of Cuba was present as there were many slave uprisings and this phase of history was responsible for the Matanzas Afro-Cuban cultural influence that remains so strong today. Many African traditions persist in the city today, which provides a lovely opportunity for immersion into a rich culture. In many ways, "being there" is the best way to "know" the culture.

Getting to The City of Matanzas

The blessing and the curse of Matanzas is the location; this lovely little city finds itself right in the middle of two locations that are much louder and often more celebrated by tourists, Havana and Varadero. Havana, as we have discussed, is the main attractions for those who crave the urban element of Cuban culture. Varadero, however, is more or less a resort area specifically for tourists. Because it is hidden away between these two popular destinations, many will end up skipping right through and do not pay the city the attention that it deserves. On the other hand, the location ends up spreading awareness about the city for those passing through on their way from

one to the other.

The location also creates the demand for many buses that will run between Havana and Varadero several times every day. Generally, this is a popular way to get to Matanzas. There are trains that run between the two areas as well, including overnight opportunities on most days.

There is also an incredibly run-down electric train that runs specifically from Havana to Matanzas that, due to the state in which it exists, is not a popular choice for many tourists who visit the area.

The most common way to get to Matanzas from abroad is by flying to Havana and choosing one of these methods of transit. Alternatively, if you do not wish to stop in Havana first, many will fly to the Juan Gualberto Gomez Airport which is located much closer to Varadero and is nestled in the province of Matanzas as well.

Varadero

Varadero is perfect for the tourist who prioritizes the comforts of "vacation" more than they care about cultural immersion. Varadero is an area that is quite exclusive, where the features of the resort

district are virtually entirely "for the tourist"-- this obviously differs from modes of operation in most of the rest of the country.

If you are looking for local eateries, museums, cultural monuments, and an idea of what typical Cuban life looks like from day to day-- you are not going to find this in Varadero. What you will find, however, is equally desirable in other ways. Beautiful Caribbean beaches, all-inclusive resorts that land

129

all over the spectrum of luxury, and Cuba's only full golf course. Yes, it may not be authentic Cuban, but it is everything that many of us envision when we picture tropical Caribbean paradise.

There is no better place for a relaxing vacation in Cuba than Varadero, as it continues to find ways to establish itself as one of the world's most iconic beach getaways. Varadero is the top spot on the Hicacos Peninsula, an iconic stretch of the Caribbean's best blonde-sand beach that runs for over 21 kilometres (13 miles) and is the shining light of

Cuba's tourism industry. You should allow yourself the luxury of being in this place.

Although areas like this often get a snobbish reception due to their aim to please tourists rather than showcase local culture, it should not be understated that tourism is Cuba's most important industry and has become an important facet of the life of Cubans as well. It is not an ancient culture but that does not diminish from the level of its significance in the country. The experience that the tourist receives in Varadero may

not be different in concept than what resort-based beach vacations in other worldly locations may offer, but the delivery by warm Cuban people may be what provides the most distinction.

Regardless, Varadero is a truly impressive bastion of tourism. There are over 60 hotels, all of the markets and shops a tourist could ever need, the opportunity to engage with popular water sports and activities, and various forms of entertainment geared towards pleasing the international combination of island-loving tourists. The beach itself is what makes Varadero remarkable, though. It goes above and beyond typical expectations.

Varadero's unique presence of Cuba is attractive to several types of tourists and should be considered whether you are looking for two weeks of constant

relaxation, or whether you are merely looking for some calm recuperation after more rugged backpacking through the rest of the country or province. Even those who are looking for an authentic taste of Cuba's genuine cultural offerings can still stand to benefit from the comforts of Varadero, which does make an entirely unmistakable and essential contribution to Cuba's appeal on the international tourism market. There is nowhere else quite like it.

10 of Varadero's Most Popular Attractions

10. Parque Josone

Parque Josone is a central hub that essentially ties the entire area together more than anything other than Varadero's uninterrupted beach. Surprisingly vibrant, the area is infused with life by local musicians, all sorts of market vendors, tropical birds, and even camel rides. This representation of Cuban culture is sculpted with precision in an effort to show a cohesive image of everything that tourists want to see and expect from Cuba. It would be tough to miss Parque Josone; anyone who explores the area will find their way to this 1st Avenue hot spot on 56th street, which pulls tourists in with magnetic vibrancy.

The park's romantic feeling may have something to do with its beautiful beginning, as it was founded by a couple, Jose and Onelia, whose names combine to give the park its name. The romance today is nurtured by violets, bridges, ponds, tropical birds like parrots and flamingos, and botanical gardens which brim with life. This beautiful green oasis is a must-see for those who have made their way to Varadero.

9. Tropicana Matanzas

A Tropicana is practically a venue for a well-defined form of Cuban cabaret that has become quite famous within the country and internationally. In Varadero, at Tropicana's such as this, the audience member is treated to a production that has been customized to please tourists and give an all-encompassing musical and dance-infused piece of entertainment. The venue is located in between the city of Matanzas and Varadero and it

promises to provide an enjoyable experience that gives a great taste of local art forms and is fully enjoyed underneath the stars in the open-air venue. For roughly $50 you will receive 90 minutes of Cuba's best, most consistent entertainment and be given the opportunity to purchase dinner and drinks, too.

8. Seafari Cayo Blanco

As far as popular day-trips and excursions in and around Varadero, there is perhaps nothing as significant as the Seafari Cayo Blanco, which is offered by Catamaran. This is a full day trip that

sails out from the beautiful Marina Chapelin and takes you through some of the Caribbean's most incredible scenery en route to Cayo Blanco. Once you have arrived in Cayo Blanco, you will be treated with opportunities to eat, dance, be entertained, drink Cuban cocktails, and enjoy the presence of one of the most popular living species: dolphins. You can choose to swim with dolphins or to watch them perform in the dolphin show during the widely beloved sunset party. The water is turquoise and matches the idealized version of Caribbean sea that so many will assume is just a figment of our collective imagination. The food is top notch-- especially the seafood. Local lobster, shrimp, squid, and many types of fish are cooked delectably.

Enjoy activities like water sports, snorkelling,

or just relaxing are made easy and accessible on the wildly gorgeous virgin beach of the island of Cayo Blanco, which is a small deserted island. It is hard to picture a more relaxing environment than

Cayo Blanco, which has been designed especially to accommodate international tourists. Don't forget to bring a towel!

7. Delfinario

This natural mangrove lagoon is the home of many dolphins in Cuba. It is located near the scenic Chapelin Marina and gives you the opportunity to watch a wonderfully entertaining dolphin show for an enjoyably affordable rate. If you are willing to pay extra, you can also choose to swim with dolphins and play with them for roughly 20 minutes. There are tour operators that include the Delfinario in their repertoire, but you can also choose to go on your own adventure to this beautiful spot that defies many of the other attractions that are so commonly associated with Varadero.

6. The City of Matanzas (and the corresponding top 10 list!)

Varadero is a close neighbour of the city of Matanzas, which we have already described and explored in detail previously in this guide. If you are looking for a city that provides more genuine Cuban life in a way that is not stylized to suit international vacationers, a trip to Matanzas is absolutely in order. Matanzas is a classic Cuban city that provides perspective into the past and present state of Cuban culture, with build-

137

ings and constructions that directly and indirectly tell the stories of the people of Cuba.

Not only this, but all of the activities on Matanza's top 10 list (also in this guide) can easily be enjoyed with a couple days in the province's capital city.

5. Villa Du Pont / Mansion Xanadu

The former home of Irenee Du Pont, this is a beautiful home that was built in 1927 as a private residence, but it has since been repurposed as the main building for the Varadero Golf Club. Whether you intend on playing a round of golf or not, this hacienda-style structure with an unmistakable green roof is worth checking out-- especially due to the indoor decor. Rustic mahogany furniture, fine Italian marble floors, high-end oil paintings, and a jaw-dropping bronze candelabra make up some of the impressive arrays of decorations which colour and infuse this old home

with regal beauty. In the basement of the building is a restaurant, "Las Americas", that is commonly regarded as one of the very best in Varadero-- but, we should mention, is also agreed upon as one of the most expensive in Varadero, as well. This is a true example of a Cuban mansion from a time when the economic disparity between the rich and poor and Cuba was far more extreme.

4. Varadero Golf Club

Well, if you are going to take a look at Villa Du Pont, may as well consider playing 18 holes too, right?

Varadero Golf Club is the only 18-hole course in all of Cuba. There is another highly regarded course in Havana that is only 9-holes. If you do not think you are good enough at golf to play a full round, consider taking a lesson or two, offered by the course itself. It is not the cheapest activity, but considering it generally takes over 4 hours, and the opportunity to play a round of 18 holes in a Caribbean paradise does not exactly arise every day (for most of us), we think the price offers a lot of value and bang for your buck.

3. Cueva de Ambrosio

Cueva de Ambrosio (the Ambrosio Cave) is an important site of archeology. Basically, the drawings and paintings on the walls of these caves offer a vivid and evocative reflection of the traditional life of the local indigenous population. Discovered in 1961, these cave images depict life in Cuba before the foreign invasion that Christopher Columbus brought along with him. This particular cave has been used for many ceremonies and was also a hideout for slaves when Cuba was suffering from the negative effects of colonialism-- it is over 300 metres long. Within the natural structure, there are 5 galleries with a total of 72 rock drawings, which culminate in creating the largest collection of Taino culture and second largest collection of Indian pictograph images in the entire Caribbean.

Watch out though, if you are afraid of bats! The little fruit bats are harmless and usually seen as cute, but we feel we should warn you of their presence in case you are afraid of such things. The bats are protected as the cave is a member of Bat Conservation International (the BCI).

At this point, most professionals believe that the images on the Cueva de Ambrosio walls are over 2000 years old. This surreal site is a treat for the mind and certainly worth checking out!

2. Reserva Ecologica Varahicacos

Cueva de Ambrosio is actually located within Reserva Ecologica Varahicacos, which was established as an ecological preserve in 1974. It isn't the largest collection of land, coming in at just 3 square-kilometres, but this protected land offers a lot

139

for the tourist, traveller, or adventure; specifically for the outdoor enthusiast. The hiking trails that cut through this plot of land, located on the north-east side of the Hicacos peninsula, offer some exciting views and act as pathways to some truly unforgettable sites. This ecological reserve features the Patriarca, which is a humongous cactus that is over 500 years old, the large Ambrosio Cave, and also another cave called the Cueva de Musulmanes. The Cueva de Musulmanes is famous for a few reasons: firstly, because some very important

fossils were found there--
human fossils of a man
whose remains are spec-
ulated and dated at some-
where between 1500 and
2500 years old. The name
'musulmanes' comes from
a group of smugglers who
used this cave as a hide-
out and a vantage point in
the 19th century.

A stark contrast from
the rest of Varadero, the
Varahicacos Ecological
Reserve offers something
that the rest of the area
simply cannot: a preservation of the unique flora and
fauna that are native to the
region, as well as a valuable glimpse at the history
of the aboriginal people

who once called the land home.

1. The Beach

Not only is Varadero beach considered to be the best attraction in the resort area of Varadero, but it is often ranked and rated as the best (or one of the best) beaches in the entire world. The white sand hits the turquoise water in a dreamy way that exudes dreamy feelings of tropical paradise. It is often argued that there is not a better spot for water sports, swimming, and simple beach relaxation in the Caribbean, if not the entire world, than Varadero beach. The beach runs for 21 km (13 miles) and is basically completely uninterrupted.

Enjoying The Province of Matanzas: The Great Outdoors

Yumuri Valley:

Equidistant between Matanzas and the nearby hub of Varadero, this little burst of nature is not one that should be overlooked by any tourist who enjoys the splendors of the outdoors. The Yumuri Valley is popular for a few reasons. The bird watching is quite exceptional in this area, in a way that is not necessarily true of most of the more popular tourist destinations in Cuba; this is especially true in the deep forests at the height of the Yumuri Valley-- specifically, the La Salina fauna area is famous for its array of beautiful birds. The valley is host to the Yumuri, Canimar, Bacunayagua rivers. If you are exploring this area, do not miss the Montemar Nature Reserve, which is large in size, and includes the largest wetland in the country. If you wind up here, you should also make sure to check out the village of Guama, the nearby crocodile breeding ground called "La Boca", and Laguna del Tesoro. This area is beloved by both hikers and bikers, with many avid cyclists choosing to take the route from Havana to Varadero, with an extended stay in Matanzas which is possibly the most well suited to those who love authentic, genuine nature.

Those who cycle often love the intense and beautiful trek between Havana and Varadero. The most popular route actually depends on skipping out on the city of Matanzas,

actually turning off of the Via Blanca freeway shortly before arriving there. Yes, about 5 kilometres (3 miles) before you arrive in the city, you will take a turn to the right, making your way onto a small road that you will see shortly after crossing the Bacunayagua River via a bridge.

There are companies that will take you on tours and treks through the best of the Yumuri Valley; an area that hides beautiful villages amongst the rolling hills, beloved beaches, and vibrant sugar fields.

One of the most popular spots is Coral Beach. Coral Beach is an incredibly unforgettable bay that offers something special to the traveller with a sense of adventure. Snorkeling is available here, and this is absolutely one of the best places in Cuba to partake in that particular activity. The reefs of coral, sponges, and many types of aquatic life (including some notably colourful fish). The Canimar River in Yumuri Valley also acts an an excellent host when it comes to excursions in watercrafts-- from handmade traditional all the way to modern motorboats. Finally, there are some of Cuba's famous caves happen to be in this area, including the distinct Saturno Cave. This is a cavern which brims with odd life, stemming from the copious amounts of water within the cave (which makes it quite unique) and the eerie presence of stalactites and stalagmites... Snorkeling is possible here, too, and voyaging through these waters to take a peak amongst this unusual setting is a perspective-widening experience, to say the least!

When you stumble into one of the local villages, there will be opportunities to eat traditional Cuban meals, visit quaint museums, and enjoy an authentic like of how the generous and loving people exist when removed from the bustling cities of Havana, Santiago de Cuba, and even Matanzas. The opportunity to traverse Yumuri Valley has a wide appeal for many types of people- just don't expect to access these treasures with a conventional car.

Getting To Varadero & Travelling Within The Province

Getting to Varadero is incredibly easy. There is a lot of infrastructure to support travelling to Varadero from Havana, as well as lots of ways to get to the various locations, such as the city of Matanzas, that lay between these two major tourism hub.

From Havana: Every day there are several different opportunities to board a bus from Havana to Varadero, and vice versa. The travel time on the road is roughly 1.5-2 hours.

From Abroad: There is an airport roughly 10 km from Varadero. Many flights from abroad will come here. Despite the short distance, a taxi cab will cost roughly $25-30. A bus to the town from the local airport, on the other hand, does not cost more than $5.

Other Areas of Interest

Holguin Province

The Province of Holguin is one that features so many of the elements that exemplify the differences and distinctions

that currently exist within Cuba, culturally, geographically, and otherwise. The land itself changes dramatically; the region ranges from hilly and mountainous to beach-filled paradise. The heavily forested and pine-filled Sierra Cristal does not seem like it is in the same province as the beaches of Guardalavaca, let alone the same province; this is, of course, not the case, and the region which features this wonderful diversity of environments is the Holguin Province.

It is often reported and mostly agreed upon, that Christopher Columbus came to shore and first

encountered the beauty of this province in 1492. At the time, the Taino natives lived in this region. Spanish colonial forces changed everything in the country, but key pieces of Taino culture has been discovered here in the Holguin Province, which is a mecca of archaeology sites that focus on the people who lived here before Columbus paved the way for the Spanish.

Politically, Holguin is of interest, as well. It is the third most populated province in Cuba, but it is not the quantity of the population of people which makes the Holguin Province significant-- it is the characteristics of a few of them. Both Fidel Castro and the man he overthrew, Fulgencio Batista, came into being in this region.

149

Today, the beautiful and secluded town of Gibara offers an authentic look at what is often considered to be "genuine" Cuban life, culture, and society. Meanwhile, Guardalavaca is geared entirely towards tourists and caters to the demands of vacationers by existing as a resort-based area.

Sancti Spiritus

Sancti Spiritus is another province in Cuba in which the capital city shares the same name as the province itself. Sancti Spiritus (the city) and Trinidad are the most significant municipalities in the region, which ranges in ecological life and environmental set-

tings: the east is filled with mangroves and swamps, the west is mountainous, the south is flat, and the Northern region features protected natural areas like wetlands, the Caguanes National Park, and the Bay of Buena Vista.

Although it is slightly off of the beaten path, tourism is still (arguably) the most important industry in the province of Sancti Spiritus.

Although the capital city has more people, Trinidad is the hub of provincial tourism-- it is a city with World Heritage designation due to the abundance of colonial buildings and a noticeable lack of buildings later than the 19th century. Other than tourism, sugar cane and cattle are agricultural contributors which have an impact on the province's economy; to a lesser extent, rice and

152

tobacco are produced as well.

The city of Sancti Spiritus is also an aesthetically pleasing and culturally rich municipality, it is just slightly edged out by Trinidad in this way. In either city, fine food, music, and architecture can easily be accessed in a relaxed and authentic way.

If you end up in the province of Sancti Spiritus, you must make your way to the Museo Nacional Camilo Cienfuegos in the town of Yaguajay. Situated just over 35 kilometres away from Caibarien, Yaguajay is a small, modest town that just happens to feature one of the best museums in all of Cuba. The museum has been operational since 1989. In many ways, the museum is quite similar to the famous Che Guevara installation that draws so much attention in Santa Clara.... Much like that monument, this museum is a tribute to a specific event that occurred in this very town, but with Camilo Cienfuegos rather than Che Guevara. On what is considering to be the "eve of the revolution", Camilo took control of some vital military barracks, which clinched a major victory for the rebel party. Behind the museum, there is a Mausoleum (Mausoleo de los Martires del Frente Norte de las Villas) which commemorates the people who died in this important battle, acting as a tribute. Museo Nacional Camilo Cienfuegos sits below a plaza which features the recognized "Senor de le Vanguardia" statue. For anybody who is interested in the life and stories of Camilo Cienfuegos, who is often overlooked in the shadow of Che Guevara, this is an amazing resource. The displays in this museum offer a comprehensive, detailed, and awe-inspiring look into the man who was Cienfuegos, as well as a lot of other pertinent information re-

153

garding the Cuban revolution. A popular installation is a renowned replica of "Dragon I" which was a small tank that had once been a tractor. The resourcefulness in militarizing this tractor to become a tank is, in many ways, iconic in how it symbolizes the way that the people came together to overthrow the government.

Pinar Del Rio

On the most western tip of Cuba, we find the province of Pinar Del Rio. Like Sancti Spiritus, the capital city of the region carries the namesake of the province. Furthermore, there is another area in the province that manages to steal the thunder from the capi-

tal due to immense cultural significance and physical beauty. In this province, tobacco is still a major industry. In many ways, Pinar Del Rio looks like an illustration of a page from a book of Cuba's past. However, the rustic imagery of the region is absolutely of the modern day. Tobacco is still grown in fields worked by men and oxen, and dried in desig-

155

nated old-school houses. The cigars you will find in Pinar Del Rio have been considered the best on the planet for some time, which is not a reputation that has faded in the eyes of many.

The land is green and lush, but some cities manage to contribute to the spark of the area, such as Valle de Viñales. Valle de Viñales is a UNESCO World Heritage Site. Unlike many other heritage sites in Cuba, this one is not preserved for its architectural impression, but for its natural beauty. This is emblematic of Valle de Viñales and Pinar Del Rio's most distinct offering to the tourist: providing the valuable experience of immersing oneself in a thriving natural environment. The town of Viñales, just north of the valley, is charming, for example, but the natural beauty of the greenery surrounding it, as well as the iconic limestone monoliths, is what makes this area appealing. Rather than

navigating loud and busy cities that pulse with lively energy, the Pinar Del Rio province offers this type of serenity; Valle de Viñales particularly includes massive caves to explore with torches and guides, typical Cuban countryside (rich with tobacco plantations), pleasant beaches that are internationally beloved, and so much more of Cuba's best and most interesting qualities.

The city of Pinar Del Rio does not stand up to many other cities in the Caribbean in terms of uptempo energy, but it stands out positively in certain ways. The architecture is attractive in a distinct way. The dance and bar scene is alive and thriving. Tobacco factories can be visited. It is a slow city that does not seem to fuss about being considered hip, urban, or metropolitan. Mostly, it is a gateway to greener pastures (literally), but time in this city can absolutely be enjoyed, as well.

The Province of Villa Clara

The province of Villa Clara is full of unexpected delights. At one point there was a larger, comprehensive province called "Las Villas" that consisted of Cienfuegos, Sancti Spiri-tus, and Villa Clara. Villa Clara has kept the identity of "Las Villas" -- so, when you hear somebody refer to "Las Villas" there is a good chance that they are referring to Villa Clara. Las Villas, of course, translates directly into "The Cities." The cities this name refers to are Trinidad, Santa Clara, Sancti Spiritus, and

San Juan de los Remedios; four of the first cities that the Spanish colonial forces created within what is now known as Cuba. The Province of Villa Clara had always been a hub of sugar production, historically and in the more recent past. After Castro overthrew the Batista regime, sugar production in this area remained prominent although the means of producing the resource were absolutely shifted. Since the 1990s, the area's main industry has been tourism, and Villa Clara has gained a reputation for fabulous beach resorts.

HASTA
LA VICTORIA

...The Province of Villa Clara: Santa Clara

Santa Clara is the capital city of Villa Clara, as it was also the capital of Las Villas as well. Santa Clara is the fifth most populated city in Cuba and offers a lot of fine attractions. The city centre is a renowned park, Parque Vidal, which is one of the more interesting and decorated parks in the country. There is an iconic statue of Marta Abreu in the park, and the park is surrounded by other monuments and structures of significance. The Santa Clara Libre is used to be a Hilton Hotel, the "Gran Hotel" is a treat for the eyes, and the Teatro de La Caridad has been declared as a national monument as Cuba. The "Plaza del Mercado Central" is a wonderful spot and the Colonia Espanola de Santa Clara is a renowned centre of dance... Basically, this park is a conglomeration of many of the province and city's most celebrated cultural offerings. Spending an afternoon in the park (Parque Vidal) will provide a fine example of typical Cuban life. You will see how locals socialize, meet, and convene. This is a lovely way to witness Cuban customs. Watch the locals blend, singles become couples, and musicians improvise away during the afternoons-- sharing their musical skills with the public.

For those interested in Che Guevara, take a moment to pay tribute to the famous revolutionary at the mausoleum in which Che and 16 of his counterparts who fought for freedom with him in Bolivia are laid to rest. During the famous "Battle of Santa Clara," the revolutionary leader Che Guevara

161

derailed a train that helped bring success and prominence to the small but significant group of socialist freedom fighters… The "Battle of Santa Clara" is considered to be the final battle of the Cuban Revolution and the one that finally destroyed Batista and his regime, paving the way for the independent socialist Castro to seize power. Che Guevara played a major role in this specific battle and he is commemorated with a monument in Santa Clara, as well as other monuments around the entire country.

> **"Battle of Santa Clara" is considered to be the final battle of the Cuban Revolution**

The Province of Villa Clara: The Cays

Villa Clara is well known for its small islands, also known as "The Cays." In this province alone, there are over 500 islands, many of which are exceedingly small and hardly utilized. Regardless, they add a special beauty to the region, and the area is also home to a large coral barrier reef which is second in size only to the famous one in Australia. Running along this reef is nearly 20 kilometres of white-sand beaches that are widely regarded as creating an utter paradise of a Caribbean tropical nature.

Together, the cays of Villa Clara combine for nearly 80,000 hectares of land and in terms of their natural cohesion: they remain largely intact. A lot of Cuba's native wildlife and plant life still bloom and live without interference on many of these small islands, including almost

162

250 species of plants which thrive to this day.

Cayo Las Brujas, Cayo Ensenachos, and Cayo Santa Maria stand out from the hundreds of islands as being particularly stunning and enjoyed by those who make their way to their virgin shores. These wildly beautiful examples of fine landscapes have become highly regarded gems of untouched Cuban brilliance. The cays can be reached through a visit to the port at Caibarien, which is a small harbor town which mostly depends on fishing.

... Getting to Villa Clara:

The city of Santa Clara has an international airport which commonly sees

163

arrivals from domestic airports and others abroad.

Gran Parque Nacional Sierra Maestra (and Comandancia de la Plata)

Home of the Campesinos (Cuba's hard-working rural population), Gran Parque Nacional Sierra Maestra is a breathtaking place. Among the most glorious areas of Cuba, the stunning mountains effortlessly contribute to one of the most amazingly lush, green, and impressive landscapes in the entire Caribbean. The sky high, humid forests of the Gran Parque Nacional Sierra Maestra create a natural sanctuary unlike any other in the country. Currently, this is an area of earnest, understated peace. In the past, the park was not immune to the tumultuous aspects of social change, and this forested park was absolutely host to the armed guerilla warfare of 1950s-era Cuba. In fact, the area contains

the previous home of the rebels who staged the successful revolution. The highest peaks in Cuba call this park home, as does a staggering amount of flora and fauna. Tall mountains, excessive humidity, and relative seclusion make this is a contrast to much of what is commonly associated with Cuba.

Deep in the trees, Comandancia de la Plata is the aforementioned previous base of the rebels. They chose this spot because it provided the ability to hide in a vast wilderness, allowing Fidel Castro and his comrades to hide away. It was never discovered by Batista and his associates, which obviously contributed to the success of the Castro-led uprising. The HQ is tucked away within the thick forests at the top of a naturally walled space atop a mountain. Today, the base has been preserved in such a way that it still gives a great vision

of what was going on at the time, in the 1950s. Casa de Fidel, which is Fidel Castro's old house, is an amazing example of strategic design; there are seven secret escape routes that would conceivably allow the leaders of the revolution to escape unharmed from a tense situation. Along with this, there are 15 other buildings (all made from wood) that were built to perform minimalistic, simple functions on the site. Being in the presence of this basic architecture, which was literally the home to the birth of some of the most important thought and strategy in the history of Cuba (and socialism in general) is humbling and powerful. Now, the area has museum-like elements, but nothing especially over the top. You will gain perspective on how the rebels

165

used radio communication through their protected communications buildings, which require a steep uphill climb to access, but still cannot be spotted from a distance. The rebels would broadcast to each other frequently. Strategically placed quite far away, well below the base camp, there are hospital buildings. These act as reminders and educators as to the roughness of the level of medical aide that was accessible at the time. The Centro de Informacion de Fora y Fauna in Santo Domingo operate, manage, and control this historical attraction. It is a 5 kilometre journey to the area from the main site and hiring a guide is essential (and required). The whole experience will not set you back too much financially, though, as the guide, transport, water, and some food comes in a package of roughly $30 CUC.

The small village of San-

to Domingo is also a place to see; the modest home of the hard-working Campesino's, it is no wonder that the people who come from this area are proud to call Santo Domingo their home. The village is an understated pleasure, far from the pressures of urban life, and instead managing to find a gentle peace within a stunning, verdant valley that is home to a crystal clear stretch of the wonderful Rio Yara. Life here has not changed very much over the years. Stepping into Santo Domingo today is not very much different, if at all, than if you had walked the humble roads of the village at the same time as historical icons and legends like Che Guevara in the middle of the 20th century. Take a look at the school and medical clinic to further your understanding of how rural society embraces and lives within socialism. Consider checking out the miniscule museum which

167

tells of the significance of this lovely little town.

Santo Domingo is the hub which acts a gateway to many of the local outdoor activities too, including hikes, horseback riding, and other expeditions.

Cuba: In Conclusion

We truly believe that Cuba has something to offer anybody and everybody.

Geographically speaking, Cuba naturally brews the recipe to concoct the best beaches in the world, which make a happy marriage with the fact that the country's temperatures manage to land within the most popular for many tourists. The climate is tropical. The social climate is friendly and warm. The seas are among the Caribbean's most appreciated and respected. The entire experience is comparably affordable when considering the prices that are paid for food, drink, transport, and more in many other countries that offer similar amenities and attractions.

There is something truly unique and special about Cuba; in fact, there are many things about the island nation which contribute to its national identity.

The cities of Havana and Santiago de Cuba burn with urban Caribbean culture. The music, dance, bars, and general infrastructure are geared toward those who are interested in an energy that buzzes and booms without becoming overwhelming; the warmth of the people of Cuba ground these wild cities in something comfortable, relatable, and welcoming. For those who are looking to try every

national food of Cuba, seek out exciting possibilities around every corner, and stumble into important cultural and historical monuments and structures at a fairly constant rate, these cities are absolutely world class.

Areas like Varadero offer some of the planet's finest beach within a community of Cubans who have constructed a community of resources and infrastructure specifically to accommodate and please those who choose to be tourists in the country. Varadero offers immense value for those looking for a vacation: it is affordable, beautiful, relaxing, and filled with all sorts of opportunities to see sights and enthusiastically en-

169

Cuba Today

gage with attractions and activities. Despite this, the opportunity to be a beach bum, strictly eat from your all-inclusive resort, and take "lounging" to the next level is also one that is provided by the generous and traveller-friendly Varadero area.

Hidden gems that blend rural life, authentic Cuban urban life, and the collective cultures which have been forced together to create "Cuba", a truly unique paradise that continues to shine with authenticity, freedom, and rebellious spirit.

So, why go now?

Cuba still stands strong and solitary as a truly remarkable destination. From our perspective, it is one of the most distinct countries in the world, in the way in which it blends so many popular elements which tourists desire and crave in one relatively small country. Cuba is a country that continues to triumph over expectations and thrive, rather than just thrive, in spite of massive political pressure and obstacles. The people of Cuba cherish and embody the creative, strong, and free spirit that Cuba has garnered through so many

years of toil, struggle, and fight for change. Cuba and its people remain buoyant in spite of everything, the rhythm of the city streets matches the beat of the local music: upbeat, exotic, alive, and infectious. The people of Cuba are typically thrilled to greet, interact, and share with visitors and tourists, as they work to make so many outsiders feel truly welcomed with warm hospitality. It is the people of Cuba that, in our opinion, make the massive contribution that truly tips Cuba into the territory of being a global elite in the tourism industry.

The Heritage Remains

A lot of the architecture that dominates Cuban cities and settlements consists of the same fortresses and structures

that have stood for hundreds of years. Most of the buildings have been repurposed in one way or another, but the same fortresses that once defended the Spanish colonialists from pirates, the same mansions that decorated capitalists once had built for them, and the same marvelous Spanish-influenced powerful city buildings still stand as they once did. Indeed, many of Cuba's most influential cities remain looking remarkably similar to the way they would have appeared hundreds of years ago. Modern Cuban culture has adapted to these fine spaces and infused classic Cuba

with new energy through meaningful social changes and developments. Central plazas surrounded by architectural wonders are surrounded by cobblestone streets which lead the traveler to all sorts of delights. Modernity has settled both in and around these traditional areas, but these cities keep a rustic appeal that cannot be replicated by new-age design. More resources are always being devoted to restoration and reclamation which rejuvenates the finer aspects of these structures and allows them to do justice to their historical precedents. Still, age does not do a disservice to these lovely old buildings

173

174

and monuments.

More Than Just Beautiful Beaches

Yes, many of Cuba's highly desired white sand beaches are involved in the conversations which debate the country with the 'best in the world'. To understate the tremendous beauty and popularity of the beaches of Cuba would be an obvious injustice. However, despite the fact that these beautiful and soothing collections of white sand and turquoise-blue water have a magnetic effect which pulls tourists from all over the planet, many visitors end up falling in love with Cuba for other reasons. Naturally, Cuba offers some fine splendors that are more-or-less unparalleled in terms of the way in which they combine. There are deep forests, wildly defined mountains, swamps which are filled with crocodiles and other life, classic Caribbean coffee and tobacco plantations (many abandoned, many operational), and everything in between. Many famed scientists and thinkers from around the globe have found themselves reaching the belief that Cuba is a marvel akin to the Galapagos, where a multitude of evolutionary oddities unite to create a Caribbean environmental reality like no other. It is our blessing as travellers to be able to enjoy the treasures that Cuba lays at our feet.

You Never Know What You Will Get

In a land where financial capital is stripped of the "be all, end all" philosophy which is generally attached to it, our expectations are constantly being challenged and tested. Modern and classic at the same time, some moments that you experience will feel as though they belong in another era-- others may feel as if they belong in another world. The embargo has been a blessing and a curse for Cuba. For the traveller who is comfortable and enthused to engage with a completely different way of approaching reality, the blessing will be felt on an exponential level.

Now Is The Time!

Right now, Cuba is in a beautiful place in terms of its society and economy. Hard communist socialism has molded to meet public demand, and certain elements of the social system have become more malleable. For example, Cuban cities are full of private restaurants and accommodation options that are just beginning to burgeon with creativity and distinction. This is a wonderful addition to traditional Cuban society. Many fear that the acceptance of free enterprise into the culture may lead to a saturation and dominance of American multinational corporations like Wal-Mart, McDonalds, and Starbucks. We certainly hope this is not the case, but there is no way to tell. Right now, however, the island nation is free of such brands, and it has allowed an ever-improving consumer culture to begin to emerge for the tourist to enjoy. It is hard to believe the nation would ever conform to certain Western ideas that would jeopardize its national identity but, still, you never know what the future holds, and the present is currently at a place that is easy to adore.

Final Checklist: The Ultimate Cuban Top 5

In this guide, we have covered most of what travellers love about Cuba. Of course, many people end up having their own beautiful experiences in the country while enjoying very little of the common attractions and carving

their own unique visit. We recognize this, while also trying to provide a universal array of options that could potentially build a strong foundation for a trip to Cuba of any length.

Of course, different people have different preferences. However, after exploring Cuba and creating this guide, we have landed on 5 broad attractions that will certainly add positive experiences to (we believe) anybody's time in the country.

5. The Architecture:

The influence of Spanish colonialism remains in a way that has been greatly changed; the symbolism has moved from that of oppression to that of liberation in the eyes of the Cubans, but the beautifully ornate architecture remains standing. Obviously, Havana and Santiago de Cuba provide amazing examples of fine Colonial architecture, as well as featuring finely designed buildings that have

developed in the hundreds of years since. Also, if you make your way to Matanzas, you will get to experience the reason why the city has been considered the "Venice of Cuba" for its rivers and bridges, and also take in the remnants of the culture which once created the reputation for Matanzas being the "Athens of Cuba."

4. The Caves of Cuba:

Known as the "Cuevos" in Cuba, the caves of Cuba have an ancient and compelling story to tell. Ambrosio Cave, Saturna Cave, and the

179

Bellamar Caves are just a few examples of caves which exemplify different elements of Cuba's natural and indigenous past.

3. The City Parks:

Parque Libertad, Parque Central, Parque Cespedes, and Parque Vidal are just a few examples we mentioned of the city parks which act as the heart of the population of each respective city in Cuba. City parks are where people socialize; playing chess, flirting, enjoying games, and listening to the fruits of the labour from the local musicians who play for their community.

2. The Beaches:

Obviously, the highlight here is the one and only Varadero Beach. This is basically 20 kilometres of the world's finest beach:

white sand, crisp turquoise water, palm trees, and many bars to grab a snack or a cocktail. The claim of "the world's finest" is a bold one, but this amazing beach in Varadero always manages to get itself involved in the conversation for this type of prestigious title. Varadero has worked to become a tourist's paradise, and it is time for you to get yourself a Pina Co-lada and bask in the glory of Varadero Beach… Still, beyond Varadero Beach, Cuba is an island in which much of the coastal perimeter would classify as a beach, and Varadero is not without elite company in this category

1. The Culture:

Wherever you go in Cuba, you will experience several elements of a very distinct but incredibly multifaceted culture. The people themselves create this, and spread the glow of Cuban warmth manifests in the food, music, dance, museum displays, public sculptures and art, and in the way the people live peacefully and happily within their natural environment. A case could be made that Cuban culture is second to none. So many styles of music, from Cuban Jazz to Rumba, have been birthed and perfected on this Caribbean island, and the cuisine continues to evolve into a major strength for the nation, after years of being considered a bit of a sore spot. Many of the museums are located within the walls of colonial-era palaces and fortresses, and so many of the distinct and truly unique aspects of Cuba which give it such a rich national identity really cannot be replicated elsewhere. To say "Cuban culture" almost seems as if it could be an oxymoron within itself, but it is not. This collection of diverse influences has converged to the point where any dusty old rustic door you choose to open could lead you to the cultural experience of a lifetime.

Picture credits

https://www.flickr.com/photos/holyfinder/favorites/
https://www.flickr.com/photos/pedrosz/
https://www.flickr.com/photos/weyes/
https://www.flickr.com/photos/pedrosz/
https://www.flickr.com/photos/budellison/
https://www.flickr.com/photos/topyti/
https://www.flickr.com/photos/dblackadder/
https://www.flickr.com/photos/romtomtom/
https://www.flickr.com/photos/84554176@N00/
https://www.flickr.com/photos/kudumomo/
https://www.flickr.com/photos/samchills/
https://www.flickr.com/photos/24580165@N03/
https://www.flickr.com/photos/kucinski/
https://www.flickr.com/photos/miguel_discart/
https://www.flickr.com/photos/dexxus/
https://www.flickr.com/photos/lexdjelectronic/
https://www.flickr.com/photos/matthiasschack/
https://www.flickr.com/photos/gemwebb/

Printed in Great Britain
by Amazon